WHO AM I?

ROBERT L THOMAS

'A refreshing Biblical approach to the psychological angst of our culture. Much Christian counseling is too influenced by Pagan thinking. Robert Thomas points us back to the Bible for our answers.'

Rev Dr. Paul Blackham
Associate Minister (Theology)
All Souls Church, Langham Place, London

'The Word of God acts like a mirror to reflect accurately the true reality of one's heart and mind—the authentic self (Prov. 27:19; Jas 1:23-25). My esteemed colleague and friend, Dr. Robert L. Thomas, explores the biblical breadth and plumbs the theological depth of what Scripture teaches about the reality of "self." With over 40 years of proven NT scholarship to his credit, Dr. Thomas correctly proposes and them compellingly details his thesis that the NT teaches a death-life paradox as the paradigm by which best to understand and live out a proper Christian self-concept. I warmly commend this work.'

Richard L. Mayhue, Th.D.
Executive Vice President,
The Master's College and Seminary, California

WHO AM I?
THE CHRISTIAN HUNGER FOR SELF-IDENTITY

ROBERT L THOMAS

MENTOR

Dedicated to the men in my discipleship labs
who, after discussing the principles outlined in this book,
were willing to put those principles into practice

© Robert L. Thomas
ISBN 1 85792 519 X

Published in 2002 by
Christian Focus Publications,
Geanies House, Fearn, Ross-shire,
IV20 1TW, Great Britain.

Edited by Lynn Quigley
Cover design by Alister MacInnes

Printed by Bell & Bain Ltd., Glasgow

Contents

Introduction

THINKING
BIBLICALLY
ABOUT
ONESELF

Who am I? Stated another way, how is a Christian t
herself? We want to address a subject that you h
about before, but we want to do so from a differen.
cultural emphasis in most of today's western world enc
to think about themselves in a certain way. Is that way in ag.
with what the Bible teaches? A series of New Testament passag.
tell how Christians should think of themselves. We want to examine
those passages, but first we need to emphasize the importance of our
minds.

1. Learning how to think

I have spent much of my life trying to teach students how to think.
That is not an easy task. People's minds are lazy and they find
thinking to be painful. All of us are that way. But God's Word
expects us as Christians to use our minds. Peter exhorts us to gird
up the loins of our minds (1 Pet. 1:13), and Paul speaks of the need
to be transformed through the renewing of our minds (Rom. 12:2)
and to be renewed in the spirit of our minds (Eph. 4:23). The Bible
also tells the kinds of things we are to think about: 'Finally, brothers,
whatever is true, whatever is honorable, whatever is right, whatever
is pure, whatever is lovely, whatever is of good reputation, if there
is any virtue and if anything worthy of praise, let your mind dwell
on these things' (Phil. 4:8). Teaching ourselves how to think is the
biggest challenge we as Christians face. It is probably the most
basic lesson of Christian living. In a world where many attractions
are vying for our attention, we need special stimuli to keep our
minds on the right subjects.

2. Learning how not to think of ourselves

Having the right thoughts is particularly important when thinking
about ourselves. Contemporary experts in psychology are
furnishing formulas prescribing how we should conceive of
ourselves. Often their answers to this challenge are the exact
opposite of what the Bible tells us to think of ourselves. Two
modern examples will illustrate.

Worm anthropology. To introduce the first example, let me use
myself as an illustration. I want you to know who I am deep inside.

. will explain why this subject is so important to me. From age to age 22 I was a deeply troubled individual. Those were the years from about the fifth grade until I graduated from college. Throughout that period I lived with a deep-seated guilt. I was worthless and I knew it. Nothing I did was right. I had a sense of responsibility to God that I could never fulfill. Beginning at age ten, I cried myself to sleep every night for many weeks and months. My parents were deeply concerned. My father was at my bedside each night to offer words of encouragement. He took me to an expensive Atlanta psychiatrist whom he could not afford, to try to get help for me. To get my mind off my problems, the psychiatrist recommended an expensive boys' club in an exclusive part of Atlanta that my parents could not afford, but they sent me anyway. The boys' club activities were outstanding, but all those activities only deadened the pain a little. They gave me no lasting relief from my deep depression. As my teen years wore on, I was as active as I could be in the liberal church to which my family belonged. I engaged in athletics and extra-curricular activities in high school. In college I stayed as busy as possible. All this kept my mind off my problem a little, but my deep-seated guilt remained. I viewed myself as a worm because that's what I was.

One branch of Christian psychologists would say I was right on target in my view of self. They would say we need to carry around guilt in everything we do. This 'worm anthropology' approach lies behind such statements as the following that come from this group of Christian counselors: 'Those of us who believe that mankind is fallen have reason to expect that much of what comes between the stimulus and the response will prove to be ugly and twisted.'[1] 'The human personality is a reservoir of the most incredible feelings and ideas' (ibid., 100). 'Sinful thoughts, words and deeds flow forth from this darkened heart automatically and compulsively, as water from a polluted fountain. The human heart is now a reservoir of *unconscious disordered motivation and response.*'[2] 'Unless we understand sin as rooted in unconscious beliefs and motives and figure out how to expose and deal with

L. J. Crabb, Jr., *Understanding People,* Grand Rapids: Zondervan, 1987, 99.
2. R. Lovelace, cited by ibid., 128

these deep forces within the personality, the church will continue to promote superficial adjustment.'[3]

What worm anthropology does not take into account is the new nature that a believer has in Christ and the opportunity for that new nature to prevail over the flesh through the enablement of the Holy Spirit (Gal. 5:16-22).

Self-exaltation anthropology. At the other extreme is the dominant advice coming from most Christian psychologists and counselors. That is to have love for myself, to have a high view of my own self-worth, a high self-esteem. Typical of this avalanche of material with which we are being bombarded is a publisher's promotion for a recent Christian book. It reads:

> Improved self-esteem leads to a true evaluation and acceptance of others and ourselves. [The author] challenges people to discover their uniqueness and to enjoy who they are. She encourages them to discover their God-designed temperament/type in order to arrive at healthy self-esteem and self-worth. This self-acceptance automatically raises the level of understanding and lowers tension in every arena and age of life, making it 'fun' to celebrate differences rather than feel obligated to think and function according to what another dictates.
>
> [This book] answers our questions regarding the differences in people by using quizzes and real-life examples sprinkled with humor. Readers will painlessly and proudly discover that their personal prefer-ences, though perhaps very different, are normal and 'ok.' Encourage-ment to join hands with God by using our special gifts to improve our spiritual confidences forms the foundation of *Self-Esteem*.[4]

In support of this position a prominent clergyman in California says that Martin Luther and the other Reformers were mistaken in building their theology around God instead of around Man. He concludes that the essence of man's problem is low self-esteem. He writes, 'I contend and plead for a full-orbed theological system beginning with and based on a solid central core of religious truth— the dignity of man. And let us start with a theology of salvation

3. Ibid., 129.
4. Web-site of Smythe and Helwys Publishing, Inc., <http://www.helwys.com/books/rward.html>, June 24, 2001)

that addresses itself at the outset to man's deepest need, the 'will to self-worth.'[5] He defines sin as 'any act or thought that robs myself or another human being of his or her self-esteem'.[6] Here are his words:

> I don't think anything has been done in the name of Christ and under the banner of Christianity that has proven more destructive to human personality and, hence, counterproductive to the evangelism enterprise than the often crude, uncouth, and unchristian strategy of attempting to make people aware of their lost and sinful condition.[7]

What self-exaltation anthropology does not take into account is Paul's admonition for a person not to think of himself/herself more highly than he/she ought to think (Rom. 12:3). Scripture observes that self-love is one of the symptoms of a degenerating society in the last days (2 Tim. 3:1-5).

Those are two examples of how not to think of ourselves: worm anthropology and self-exaltation anthropology. Both are wrong paths to follow toward achieving a biblical view of self.

3. Learning how to think accurately about ourselves

How can we think honorable, pure, and lovely things about ourselves as Philippians 4:8 instructs? How can we have thoughts of good reputation that are virtuous and worthy of praise when the object of our thinking is ourselves? The New Testament provides consistent teaching to provide an answer to this question. The string of passages begins with Matthew and goes all the way through Revelation. For too long this teaching in the Bible has not received the attention it should. The current focus on self in our world community requires us to re-examine the Scriptures to find out how we should view ourselves. I have three reasons for thinking this need is so great.

(1) The first one is personal. The personal problems I had when

5. Robert H. Schuller, *Self-Esteem: The New Reformation* [Waco, Tex.: Word, 1982], 150.
6. ibid., 14.
7. Robert Schuller, 'Dr. Schuller Comments' in Letters to the Editor, *Christianity Today* [October 5, 1984]: 12.

I was young is a good enough reason for me. I was so introspective that I was overcome with guilt in considering my many failings. My biggest need was to receive Christ who died to take away sins and to realize His forgiveness, which I eventually did. But beyond that conversion experience my introspection continued. How was I to think of myself as a Christian? Early in my Christian experience an older Christian shared Romans 12:3 with me, a verse that said I should not think more highly of myself than I ought to think. He used the verse to prove to me that I should think favorably of myself. Even in my brief Christian walk up to that point, that didn't sound like the right interpretation of the verse. I still needed an answer.

(2) Another reason for pursuing the biblical teaching on self-concept is the primacy that Jesus gave the subject in His ministry. For Him it was an indispensable consideration. Jesus made it perfectly clear that this line of thinking is the absolutely necessary first step to becoming His disciple. Without it there can be no lasting discipleship. We will have more to say about this when we look at the five occasions in the Gospels where Jesus taught His disciples and others about how to think of themselves.

(3) A third reason for the need to learn how to think about oneself is the obvious fact that how we think about ourselves determines how we respond to various life-situations. How we respond in turn determines how effective we are in our service for Christ. The Christian way of self-definition will save us from those outlandish moments when we have nothing good to say for ourselves. It will also save us from those preposterous times when we are on top of the world and nothing seems beyond our reach, when our self-esteem is at record-high levels. It will keep us in touch with our Lord and Savior no matter what difficult decision we may face. It will lay the foundation for a lasting commitment to His service. It is the irreplaceable starting point for a life of devotion. The genuineness of Christian commitment depends solely on a Christian view of self. Self-concept is the only lasting basis for dedicating ourselves to God.

It is not enough just to think of ourselves. We must follow the biblical pattern in doing so.

4. Learning how to think accurately and paradoxically about ourselves

Thinking paradoxically about ourselves is nothing new to Bible students, but it is a new way of expressing familiar biblical teaching. Putting together a string of familiar, similar passages brings us to an inevitable conclusion that has escaped wide attention. The way we are to think of ourselves is a biblical paradox, a contradiction, an incongruity, an oxymoron. The New Testament consistently instructs us to think of ourselves as *living corpses*. We are dead and therefore in a sense corpses, yet we are alive and so we are living. For me to speak of myself as a living corpse is an oxymoron, a contradiction in terms. Secular common sense tells me that a person cannot be dead and alive at the same time. But biblical common sense tells me otherwise. Because a believer in Christ is identified with Christ in His death and identified with Him in His resurrection, he/she is both dead and alive. Christians operate in a realm different from that of non-Christian earthlings and are not subject to usual rules of secular logic. The New Testament teaches unequivocally about the death-life paradox in Christian self-concept.

When He was on earth as a man, the God-man Jesus introduced this paradoxical way of thinking. The Gospel of Matthew tells when He initiated it, and John in the Book of Revelation shows that the paradox will still be valid for Christians in the future, just before Jesus returns to earth. In Matthew 10:39 Jesus said, 'He who has found his life will lose it, and he who has lost his life for My sake will find it.' In that statement He uses 'life' in two different senses, the first to refer to earthly, temporal life and the second— represented by the word 'it' in both parts of the statement—to refer to eternal, spiritual life. In the last half of the verse, losing life in the former sense enables a person to find life in the latter sense if he/she loses the former life for Jesus' sake. One must lose life—that is, he must die—in order to find life. That is incongruous from a human standpoint, but it is a basic fact from the biblical standpoint. In Revelation 12:11 John writes about the faithful saints in the end times: 'They did not love their life even to death.' Here he alludes to Jesus' line of teaching about earthly, temporal life.

Because of values higher than those of this world, those heroes of the future will readily surrender their lives on this earth in view of the value of obtaining a higher existence for eternity.

Between Matthew and Revelation we have such statements and commands as, 'Reckon yourselves to be dead to sin, but alive to God' (Rom. 6:11); 'One died for all, therefore all died; and He died for all, that they who live should no longer live for themselves, but for Him who died and rose again' (2 Cor. 5:14-15); 'I have been crucified with Christ; and it is no longer I who live, but Christ lives in me' (Gal. 2:20); 'You have died with Christ to the elementary principles of the world. . . . You have been raised up with Christ' (Col. 2:20; 3:1); 'We know that we have passed out of death into life' (1 John 3:14); and a number of others. Such passages illustrate the importance of the biblical self-concept for every situation in life.

How we think has everything to do with how we behave. Specifically this is true in regard to how we think about ourselves. It is of ultimate importance in our relationship with God and with one another. It is of ultimate importance in our service to God and to one another.

The chronological order in which the New Testament presents this subject does not lend itself to an easy apprehension of the concept, so we will put the passages in a sequence that begins with the most direct and succinct statements of how a Christian should think of himself/herself and continue passage by passage in a non-chronological sequence. Sometimes the concept comes by way of a direct command to readers; at other times the experience of Jesus, Paul, or someone else illustrates the concept. Whether the view of self is taught by direct command or by personal illustration will be obvious in each case.

The following discussions show the critical importance of the death-life paradox in a Christian's view of self in various phases of responsibility. They will deal with a Christian's view of self in

(1) 'Overcoming Sin's Domination' (Rom. 6:1-14)
(2) 'Gaining Freedom from Law' (Galatians 2:19-20)
(3) 'Counteracting Wrong Rules' (Colossians 2:20–3:16)

(4) 'Evaluating Family Ties' (Matthew 10:37-39)

(5) 'Suffering with Christ' (Matt. 16:24-26 = Mark 8:34-37 = Luke 9:23-25)

(6) 'Evaluating Earthly Possessions' (Luke 14:26-27)

(7) 'Responding to This World's Allurements' (Luke 17:32-33)

(8) 'Fruit-bearing for God' (John 12:24-26)

(9) 'Fulfilling a Broad Range of Christian Responsibilities' (Romans 12:1-2)

(10) 'Failing Successfully' (2 Corinthians 4:7-15)

(11) 'Succeeding Successfully' (Philippians 3:2-16)

(12) 'Persuading Others to Believe in Christ' (2 Corinthians 5:11-21)

(13) 'Ridding Oneself of the Hideous Past' (Ephesians 4:17-24)

(14) 'Achieving Christian Submission' (1 Peter 2:24)

(15) 'Following God's Will' (1 Peter 4:1-6)

(16) 'Cultivating Love' (1 John 3:14)

(17) 'Facing Martyrdom' (Revelation 12:11).

We know how important the death and the resurrection of Jesus Christ are to our faith. The biblical self-concept provides a way we can make those two events in His experience a part of our moment-by-moment experience from day to day, that is, by continually contemplating our identification with Him when He died and when He rose from the dead. Let's get on with our survey of this theme.

Scripture translations throughout this work are those done by the author, but should be closely compatible with whatever Bible Version the reader is accustomed to.

Chapter 1

Overcoming Sin's Domination

Romans 6:1-14

Romans 6:1-14

[1]*What shall we say then? Should we continue in sin that grace might abound? [2]May it not happen! How shall we who died to sin live in it any longer? [3]Or do you not know that as many of us who were baptized into Christ Jesus were baptized into His death? [4]Therefore we were buried with Him through baptism into death, that as Christ was raised from the dead through the glory of the Father, so we also might walk in newness of life. [5]For if we have been united with Him in the likeness of His death, certainly we shall be also in the likeness of His resurrection, [6]knowing this, that our old man was crucified with Him, that the body of sin might be done away with, that we should no longer be slaves to sin; [7]for the one who has died is freed from sin. [8]Now if we died with Christ, we believe that we shall also live with Him, [9]knowing that Christ, having been raised from the dead, dies no longer; death is no longer His master. [10]For the death that He died, He died to sin, once for all; but the life that He lives, He lives to God.*

[11]*So also consider yourselves to be dead to sin, but alive to God in Christ Jesus.*

[12]*Therefore stop letting sin reign in your mortal body so that you obey its lusts, [13]and stop presenting the members of your body to sin as instruments of unrighteousness; but present yourselves to God as those alive from the dead, and your members as instruments of righteousness to God. [14]For sin shall not be your master, for you are not under law, but under grace.*

Romans is a book of the New Testament that is full of doctrine, probably more so than any other book in the Bible. It sets forth the system of beliefs which constitute Christianity. Yet it is as practical as any book in the Bible too. Among its many teachings are two that every person should know about. The first teaching is that every person can and should escape sin's punishment. Paul, the author of Romans, covers that point particularly in Romans 3:21-26 where he speaks of Jesus Christ's death as satisfying the demands of God's wrath against sin and sinners and as providing redemption from sin's consequences, making possible a person's being declared righteous before God. A person must believe in Jesus Christ to receive this benefit.

The second teaching is that every person can and should escape sin's control. The author writes on this subject particularly in Romans 6:1-14. In this section he points to the spiritual union of a believer with Christ when Christ died, was buried, and was raised from the dead. Any person who views himself/herself realistically recognizes that he/she is a slave of sin. Sin is the master who dictates life's choices in determining one's attitudes and activities. Through the first man Adam sin entered the human family (Rom. 5:12) and has continued its domination ever since then. Through Adam's transgression, death—both physical and spiritual—became the lot of every person (Rom. 5:15). Yet the good news is that through the death of Christ people can receive 'the abundance of grace and the gift of righteousness' (Rom. 5:17). They receive the abundance and the gift when they trust Christ in escaping the penalty of sin.

That superabounding grace of Christ (Rom. 5:20-21) raises another issue for the forgiven sinner, however. Is he to keep on sinning after being forgiven, thereby magnifying the grace of God (Rom. 6:1)? Such is the question Paul answers in Romans 6:1-14. In answering this question he explains the freedom from sin's domination available to believers in Christ, and in doing so, furnishes what is probably the most succinct biblical directive of the Christian view of self and how that way of thinking frees a person from obeying sinful inclinations. We can probably best follow Paul's logic by using a second-person format to state three facts and two responses to those facts.

Three facts

Fact number one: You died

No matter what your name, what your age, where you live, on the fourteenth day of the Hebrew calendar month Nisan in the year AD 30 you died. You had not been born at that time, but in the pre-planning of God He included you among those who experienced death. One Person died that day, but His death was a 'package' transaction. He embodied everyone who has ever lived or who will ever live in the death that He died. Just as Adam's disobedience of God's command plunged the whole human race into a sinful state, so Jesus Christ's submission to God's will created a potential for all to obtain righteousness (Rom. 5:19). To create that possibility, He had to die in your place. Just as Adam is the head of a physical race of people, so the Son of God is the head of a spiritual race. Whatever happened to Him that day happened to every member of that race.

Your being 'in Christ' speaks of your uniting with Him in a spiritual sense, sometimes called a 'mystical union' because it is beyond your ability as a human being to explain. When you trusted Him for your salvation, this union occurred, and because it occurred, you became a participant in His death. Notice how Paul emphasizes your death through repetition of the fact:

Romans 6:2: 'We who died.'
Romans 6:3: 'All of us have been baptized into His death.'
Romans 6:4: 'We were buried with Him through baptism into death.'
Romans 6:5: 'We have become united with Him in the likeness of His death.'
Romans 6:6: 'Our old man was crucified with Him.'
Romans 6:8: 'We have died with Christ.'

Incidentally, the baptism spoken of in Romans 6:3, 4 is a spiritual act performed by God, not the ordinance of water baptism.

The fact is, you became an active participant in that AD30 death the moment you trusted Christ. You have been dead ever since then. Of course, your death with Christ has nothing to do with your physical being. It is simply a shift in status as God sees you. He viewed

His Son as dying the death of many people, because the death He died, He died in the place of others. So, as far as God is concerned, you are now a dead person.

Fact number two: Death frees a person from sin's control
Corpses do not sin. Adam and Eve were sinless until they yielded to the serpent's suggestion to eat the forbidden fruit. Jesus Christ was sinless throughout His life. Aside from these three people, the only others who do not sin are dead people. A cemetery is a sinless community. The slave-master sin has absolutely no claim on a dead person.

As long as you live, you can never successfully break the authority that sin has over you. The only thing that can release you from that servitude is death. When someone dies, the master-slave relationship comes to an end.

Thus your death with Christ has terminated your subservience to sin, as Paul emphatically asserts:

Romans 6:2: 'How shall we who died to sin still live in it?'
Romans 6:6: 'Our old man was crucified that we should no longer be slaves to sin.'
Romans 6:7: 'He who has died is freed from sin.'
Romans 6:10: 'The death that He died, He died to sin.'

From God's perspective, sin no longer has a claim on your life. It is impossible for sin to control you because dead people don't sin. The fact of your death with Christ frees you and lays the foundation for your experience of living without that kind of authority hanging over your head.

That fact poses a dilemma for you, however. You died when Christ died and death brings an end to sin's rule. Why then do you find yourself still struggling with temptation? The answer lies in acknowledging that until the time of his physical death, a Christian has two lives, one in this world as he has always known it and another in a spiritual sense that is not visible but is nevertheless quite real. Your ongoing struggle with temptation stems from the life still lived in this world. To the extent that you cater to that former life, you will allow sin to remain as the dominant force in your life. This approach to living advocates that the only way to get rid of temptation is to yield to it. As long as you limit your perspective to visible life as most people know it, that is an accurate statement. When you yield to that temptation, however, there will be at least ten more to take its place.

But that perspective is not accurate when you expand your vision to see the spiritual side of your existence. By concentrating on your death with Christ you can conquer temptation without yielding to it. When you do this, you free yourself from sin's power over you. Someone has said, 'When you flee temptation, be sure you don't leave a forwarding address.' Translated into terms of Romans 6, that tells you not to let your attention drift back to the old perspective when Christ was not at all in the picture. Whatever perspective you cultivate will be the one that will prevail. If you favor the old life, sin will rule. If you count on the death of the old man with Christ, you will be free from sin.

Suppose you had two pets, one that you treasure very highly and another that you detest. If you feed and favor the one and neglect the needs of the other, one will thrive and the other will eventually die of starvation. The pet that you treat with tenderness and care will prevail over the other. Your nurture of the new man who was raised with Christ should overshadow your care for the old man. Then you will have grounds for dismissing sin's authority over your decisions.

Fact number three: Life after death is Christ's life, not yours
Just as you died Christ's death, you also rose from the dead in His resurrection. The nature of your spiritual union with Him means that whatever happened to Him happened to you also. Consequently, you are a living dead person.

Just as Paul emphasizes your death with Christ, he emphasizes your resurrection with Him also:

> Romans 6:4: 'As Christ was raised . . ., we should walk in newness of life.'
> Romans 6:5: 'We have become united with Him in the likeness of His resurrection.'

Romans 6:8: 'We believe that we shall also live with Him.'

Romans 6:9: 'We know that since Christ has been raised from the dead, He no longer dies, death no longer exercises lordship over Him.'

Romans 6:10: 'The life that He lives, He lives in relation to God.'

Christ has replaced that old ego with which you were all too familiar. His resurrection life now flows through you. Paul said it this way in Galatians 2:20: 'I have been crucified with Christ; and I no longer live, but Christ lives in me.'

You died but you rose from the dead. The 'you' who now lives is not the 'you' who existed before death. The new 'you' walks in newness of life because you have been identified with Christ in His life after death. A further step in analyzing the new 'you' reveals that Christ lives His life in you through the Holy Spirit whom Christ sent. Romans 8:2, 9-11 speaks of this: 'The Law of the Spirit of life in Christ Jesus has freed you from the law of sin and death. . . . You are not in the flesh but in the Spirit, if indeed the Spirit of God dwells in you. Now if anyone does not have the Spirit of Christ, he does not belong to Him. But if Christ is in you, though your body is dead because of sin, yet the Spirit is life because of righteousness. Now if the Spirit of the one who raised Jesus from the dead dwells in you, the one who raised Christ from the dead will also make alive your perishable bodies through His Spirit who dwells in you.' The life of Christ currently finds its reality in you through the indwelling Spirit. That same life will eventually issue in resurrection life when Christ returns, when your perishable human body no longer exists.

You may retain the same name on your driver's license, but the spiritual reality is that the identity that used to reside in your body does so no longer. The new resident in your body is none other than Jesus Christ Himself. The kind of life that you now live possesses a quality different from the life you lived before. The new life is a resurrection kind of life that will never end, the kind of life that cannot commit sin. One year, my sister sent me a birthday card with a message that said, 'Don't think of it as getting one year older; think of it as getting one year closer to perfection.' When Christians experience physical death, they embark upon resurrection life as Christ did, life in its fullness in which sinning is impossible. That is the perfection the card spoke about. What the card did not say was that the potential for freedom from sin in this present life exists if we could avoid spiritual lapses, because Christians possess that resurrection life already. The problem is, of course, is that none of us avoids those lapses.

Those are the three facts: you died, death frees a person from sin's control, and life after death is Christ's life, not yours. The three facts do not answer all the questions, however. If you died and death frees you from sin's control, why do you find yourself still yielding to the rulership of sin? If the Holy Spirit is living the life of Christ through you, why does the old man still seem to be alive and well? We must look at two responses to the facts to answer those questions.

Two responses

Response number one: You must adopt those facts as your own mode of thinking

Romans 6:11 tells you how to activate the three facts stated repeatedly in Romans 6:1-10. It commands you, 'Look upon yourselves as dead to sin, but alive to God in Christ Jesus.' Above, I have rendered the imperative verb stating the command as 'look upon,' but it lends itself to a variety of equivalent translations in English: 'consider,' 'reckon,' 'draw the conclusion that,' 'count,' 'think of,' 'regard,' 'deem,' 'judge,' and other similar words and expressions. 'Contemplate this picture of yourself' is the idea. 'Focus on' or 'give your continual attention' is what the command is enjoining. The whole family of words and expressions speaks of forming a mental concept. The apostle commands the Roman readers and all other believers including yourself to think of themselves in a certain way. He urges you to think of yourself in terms of the spiritual realities, i.e., the facts just disclosed in the ten previous verses. This is to be your view of self.

That Paul did not use such a word as 'imagine,' 'assume,' 'fantasize,' 'suppose,' 'theorize,' or 'conjecture' is of utmost importance. The union with Christ is not just a figment of your imagination. It does not exist only in your subjective conceptualization. Your death, burial, and resurrection with Him are objective spiritual realities. You are thinking about events that actually happened and letting your mind dwell on them. In your waking moments of consciousness, you are retaining the memory of your death, consequent release from the slavery to sin, and subsequent becoming a channel for Christ's resurrection life.

If that resurrection life fails to show itself and you find yourself serving sin once again, you have allowed your attention to revert to the old pattern according to which you thought in terms only of physical and material realities. You have become lax in focusing on spiritual facts as God sees you. As long as your mind is on the right set of realities, sin cannot have its way with you. The critical issue is obedience to the words of Romans 6:11 and thinking the right thoughts about yourself.

Romans 6:10 reveals that once for all Christ died in relation to sin. This means that He took our sin upon Himself and then separated Himself from its authority through death. Romans 6:11 tells you that you are to do the same, separate yourself from it through His death, not your own. **Romans 6:10** says that in His resurrection life Christ lives in relation to God. Romans 6:11 compares your resurrection life to His by saying yours should be in relation to God like His. God views you as a dead person who has been raised from the dead because you are 'in Christ Jesus.' Your union with Him is so close that whatever happened to Him happened to you also.

A number of possible hindrances to thinking of yourself in this way come to mind:

1. Distractions. At the beginning of the twenty-first century a fast-moving society offers many attractions that compete for your attention. Letting one or a number of these occupy your mind, though they may not seem bad in themselves, can keep you from contemplating the spiritual reality of your death and resurrection with Christ.

2. Ignorance. You may not have known the spiritual facts that govern how to think of yourself. No one has ever pointed them out to you.

Much publicity given to thinking about yourself in other ways may have drowned out the true message about the Christian view of self.

3. Weak faith. You may have known how to regard yourself, but have trouble believing it, because spiritual truths lie in the realm of the unseen. You tend to rely on things you can see with your physical eyes more than what you cannot see.

4. Forgetfulness. You may have known the truths about your identification with Christ, but with the demands of other responsibilities you may have forgotten to apply them to your own situation.

5. Unwillingness. You may love that old ego so much that you don't want to let it go. You love the pleasures of sin so strongly that you intentionally push aside your spiritual death and resurrection with Christ in deference to gratification of fleshly desires. You want to keep on feeding the old self and building it up. If this is your situation, you may begin to wonder how real your conversion to Christ was, because you obviously are choosing self over Christ. If you keep on doing this, you will certainly reap misery, defeat, slavery to sin, and no telling what else from the punishing hand of God. If, however, you prefer Christ and your union with Him over self, you are a winner, freed from sin for the enjoyment of His resurrection life.

Secular morality tells you to become what you ought to be, but the proper Christian view of self tells you to become what you already are in Christ. Christ has already won victory and liberation from sin. All you have to do is to accept it and keep on contemplating it.

Response number two: Based on your Christian self-concept, you must commit to serving God, not sin
Paul continues his instructions to the Roman readers and the rest of us with other commands in Romans 6:12-14:

Therefore stop letting sin reign in your perishable body that you should obey its lusts, and stop presenting your members to sin as instruments of unrighteousness, but present yourselves to God as those alive from the dead and your members as instruments of righteousness to God. For sin will not be lord over you, for you are not under law, but under grace.

'Therefore' at the beginning of verse 12 shows that he bases these commands on the view of self he has commanded in verse 11. Two of the new commands are prohibitions to stop allowing sin to reign as king in your life and to stop allowing the use of the members of your body for unrighteous purposes. The one positive command is to commit yourself to God and to commit the members of your body to righteous purposes. Rather than providing a license for you to keep on sinning, grace has provided for your co-death, co-burial, and co-resurrection with Christ, something that the law could not do.

As reflected in the verb tense used, Romans 6:13b speaks of a once-for-all presentation of oneself to God. It is a decisive moment when a believer decides to let God have complete charge of his life. That personal commitment to God must have a solid foundation. Otherwise, it will last only briefly. To be lasting, it must be based on the right view of self. As Paul spells out the concept so clearly in Romans 6:1-11, that concept entails a death-life paradox. You must think of yourself as dead in certain respects, those phases of your life where you have yielded and are still inclined to yield to sinful inclinations. Death to those inclinations is a historical fact even though it is spiritual in nature. When Christ died, you died.

At the same time, however, you must think of yourself as alive in certain other respects. You have become a channel for the resurrection life of Christ which sets your inclinations toward God and righteous purposes. The beginning of that resurrection life is also a spiritual, historical fact, because when Christ rose from the dead, so did you.

As you gear your thoughts about yourself this way, the result will be a committed life that no longer moves in the direction that the old master dictates. It will move in the direction of God and His values.

The inevitable

Paul has used three facts and two responses to lay out in a masterful manner the plan for escaping the domination of sin in a Christian's personal life. Following this plan will lead inevitably to Christian service for righteousness, sanctification, and conformity to the example of Christ Himself.

Years ago, I learned about a Christian student who had cheated on an examination I had given to one of my classes. I confronted the student with the evidence that had been given me by his fellow students. He broke down in tears and confessed his sin and his willingness to take whatever consequences were necessary to atone for his wrongdoing. What had happened in that student's life is that his goal was to pass the course, no matter what it took to do so. With that goal in mind, he had forgotten that the part of his person with that kind of motivation had died when Christ died and that the part who was raised with Christ would never have considered doing what is dishonest. His view of self was faulty (see Rom. 6:11) and he had therefore yielded himself to unrighteousnes instead of to God (Rom. 6:12-13).

On another occasion, one of my students was scheduled to receive an award for excellence, but he volunteered that someone in the records office had miscalculated his grade and that he did not deserve the award after all. In his case, no one besides himself and the Lord knew about the mistake. By coming forward to point out the error, this student recognized that the part of him that wanted to keep the mistake a secret so that he could receive public recognition as an outstanding student had died with Christ. He also realized that the part of him that was raised with Christ (Rom. 6:11) could only do one thing: that is, call attention to the mistake. In that instance he yielded himself to God rather than sin (Rom. 6:12-13). Freedom from sin's domination is available for the taking to the child of God.

The following chart summarizes the discussion above and emphasizes the critical importance of the death-life paradox in Christian self-concept:

Step #3: Your Decision (6:12-14):	Based on Your Christian Self-Concept, You Must Commit to Serving God, Not Sin		
Step #2: How You View Reality (6:11):	You Must Adopt Those Facts as Your Own Mode of Thinking–A Death-Life Paradox in Christian Self-Concept		
Step #1: How God Views Reality (6:1-10):	You Died	Death Frees a Person from Sin's Control	Life after Death is Christ's life, not yours

Chapter 2

Freeing Believers From The Law's Restrictions

Galatians 2:19-20

Galatians 2:19-20

[19]For through the Law I died to the Law, so that I might live to God. [20]I was crucified with Christ; and I no longer live, but Christ lives in me; and the life that I now live in the flesh, I live by faith in the Son of God who loved me and gave Himself for me.

Continuing our survey of the death-life paradox, we come next to Galatians 2:19-20. There Paul wrote, 'Through the law I died to the law that I might live to God. I have been crucified with Christ, and I no longer live, but Christ lives in me. And the life that I now live in the flesh, I live through faith in the Son of God who loved me and gave Himself for me.' In this short span Paul speaks of his own death three times: 'I died . . . I have been crucified . . . I no longer live.' He speaks of his ongoing life four times: 'that I might live . . . Christ lives in me . . . the life that I now live . . . I live.' His co-death and co-resurrection with Christ are clearly the focus of attention as he deals with a certain issue.

The Problem of Table Fellowship of Jews with Gentiles

What was that issue? The Galatian churches to whom Paul wrote had fallen prey to false teaching that advocated both faith in Christ and keeping the Mosaic law as necessities for earning salvation. To correct that error, Paul confronted Peter over a grave error committed by Peter when the two men met at Antioch in Syria between Paul's second and third missionary journeys (see Acts 18:22-23). A good number of Gentiles along with some of Jewish background composed the Christian church in that city, creating an environment for Peter's error. Paul described that encounter with Peter:

> And when Cephas [i.e., Peter] came to Antioch, I resisted him to his face, because he stood condemned. For before certain ones came from James, he was eating with the Gentiles, but when they came, he withdrew and separated himself, fearing those of the circumcision. And the rest of the Jews joined in his hypocritical act so that even Barnabas was carried away with their hypocrisy. But when I saw that they were not walking straight with the truth of the gospel, I said to Cephas before all, 'If you being a Jew live like a Gentile and not like a Jew, how do you compel the Gentiles to live like Jews?' (Gal. 2:11-14).

God had already taught Peter an important lesson in Caesarea when He led him to the house of the Gentile centurion Cornelius (Acts 10:9-29). Presumably from that point on he had no hesitancy about eating with Gentiles and was doing so in Antioch until he came under pressure from Jewish Christians who held that the Mosaic restrictions against such a practice were still in effect for Christians of Jewish background. Their conversion to Christ, they said, did not alter that Mosaic stipulation. When that pressure came, Peter reversed himself and withdrew from table fellowship with Gentile believers in Antioch (Gal. 2:11-12). Other Jewish believers, including Barnabas, followed his example (Gal. 2:13). Paul firmly condemned the action of Peter and the others as blatantly wrong, pointing out to Peter his inconsistency. At one point, Peter had terminated his compliance with Jewish restrictions and had begun living as a Gentile. By reversing himself, he was now forcing Gentiles to live like Jews if they wanted to fellowship with him around the table (Gal. 2:14). That combination of actions was indefensible.

Paul recognized the difference in background between Jews and Gentiles, but reminded Peter and his readers that even those of Jewish lineage were not justified by works of the law. They like Gentiles received Christ's imputed righteousness only through faith in Christ (Gal. 2:15-16). If seeking to be justified in Christ caused Jews to become sinners like the Gentiles when they forsook the law's restrictions, that did not make Christ a minister of sin (Gal. 2:17). To do what Peter did in submitting himself to the legal restrictions after being freed from them was in essence building again the things he had once destroyed. By that course of action a person becomes a transgressor of the law by admitting that what he did initially in forsaking the law was a violation of the law (Gal. 2:18). That was Peter's status.

Paul explains his own situation, that he is not such a transgressor. He did not forsake the law and then return to it like Peter. Through law he died to the law that he might live to God (Gal. 2:19). When he forsook the law, he did so permanently. The law's restrictions such as not eating with Gentiles no longer apply to a dead person. Paul died never to return to the law's restrictions, but in lieu of that former life under law he was now living to God.

He goes on to explain that paradox in terms of his co-crucifixion with Christ and the cessation of life for that 'I' who lived under law (Gal. 2:20a, 20b). In place of that old 'I,' Christ now lives within him (Gal. 2:20c), and the life that he now lives in the flesh is a life supported by his faith in the Son of God who loved him and gave Himself for him (Gal. 2:20d, 20e).

A similarity to Paul's words in **Romans 6:14** comes to mind. There he made the point that our death and resurrection with Christ means that we are not under law, but under grace. In Romans 6 the great liberation was our freedom from sin as a slave-master and a newfound opportunity to present ourselves in submission to God. Here his point is that our death with Christ means a freedom from the law's restrictions and the opportunity to fellowship freely around the table with those who trust Christ, regardless of whether they are Jews or Gentiles. The law's tenets are no longer binding on Christian Jews because of their death with Christ. The life of Christ through them has replaced that old life that was subject to the law's limitations.

The problem of table fellowship with Gentiles was a serious one for the early church, which in the beginning was largely a Jewish church. The earliest Christians, including the twelve apostles of Jesus, had a Jewish upbringing and had been taught all their lives to be closely observant of the law's requirements. When Christ came and fulfilled the law's requirements for Christians, the earliest Jewish believers could not grasp their new relationships with the law right away. They needed time and special revelation such as God gave Peter in sending him to the house of Cornelius, the Gentile centurion, and such as God gave Paul in epistles like Romans and Galatians. They could not assimilate all these changes at once.

Another related issue was the requirement of circumcision of males under the law. Must Gentiles undergo this rite to be saved? That was the issue that prompted the convening of the Jerusalem council described in Acts 15:4-21 and Galatians 2:1-10. Some have thought that the Acts 15 council dealt with the issue of table fellowship, but it did not. That council settled the issue that Gentiles need not be circumcised to be saved. That decision indirectly precipitated the table-fellowship debate, however. The dominantly Jewish church in Jerusalem interpreted the council's decision to mean that though Gentiles need not undergo circumcision, Jewish

Christians still had to abide by the standards of the Mosaic law, including the one that prohibited Jews from eating at the same table with Gentiles. The law contained certain dietary restrictions (Lev. 11:4; 20:25; Deut. 14:3, 7) that Jews would presumably violate if they ate with Gentiles. Jews of New Testament times interpreted the restrictions and other parts of the law to exclude their contact with non-Jews (John 4:9; 18:28; Acts 11:3; Gal. 2:12). According to the Jerusalem Christians those limitations on Jewish conduct would still be in effect in spite of the ruling on Gentile circumcision.

For Paul and his Gentile converts, however, the decision of the Acts 15 council had a different meaning. They interpreted the decision about Gentile freedom from having to be circumcised to mean that freedom from the law's restrictions extended to everyone, including Jews. Paul's critics probably accused him of inconsistency, because later he had Timothy—whose mother was a Jew and father a Greek—circumcised (Acts 16:1-3), but he had refused to compel Titus to be circumcised when the issue became a doctrinal one at the Jerusalem council (Acts 15:1-5; Gal. 2:3). Paul's answer to them lay in the differing reasons for circumcising the two men. With Timothy, as a member of Paul's traveling team, it was to keep his uncircumcised state from offending Jews whom Paul sought to evangelize; with Titus, as a primary exhibit at the Jerusalem council, it was a concession to Judaizers who contended that Gentiles had to be circumcised to be saved. Paul was unwilling to make the latter concession.

Paul's interpretation of the council's decision permitted Jewish Christians to associate freely with Gentile Christians, including around the table for meals. The interpretation of the dominantly Jewish church in Jerusalem did not.

The conflict in interpretations of the council's decision came to a head when Paul confronted Peter at Antioch. The Holy Spirit obviously endorsed Paul's interpretation of the decision by preserving his perspective on the pages of Scripture. Paul fortifies his position in Galatians 2:19-20 by pointing out the reason for his freedom from the Mosaic restrictions: the law is binding on a person only as long as he lives. Once he dies, its statutes no longer apply to him. Since Paul was crucified with Christ, the legal restrictions on associations with Gentiles no longer applied to him or any Jewish Christian. All were now free to demonstrate unity in the body of Christ in all types of associations and activities. Christ now lived in him and them just as He did in Gentile Christians.

The sufficiency of faith

Paul's Galatian readers needed to learn from Peter's mistake. They like Peter were inclined to mix works in obedience to the law with faith as a means for earning God's approval. Paul has to remind them that they received the Spirit through the hearing of faith, not through works of law (Gal. 3:2) just as he reminded them that justification was through faith without works of law (Gal. 2:16). The false teachers, called Judaizers, had tried to convince them that faith in Christ alone was not enough and along with that faith they needed to add beneficial elements by obeying the law.

They wanted to compel Gentile converts to Christianity such as Titus to be circumcised (see Gal. 2:3) because Gentile converts to Judaism had to be circumcised. Paul had to remind them that the council in Jerusalem decided against imposing that responsibility on Gentiles (Gal. 2:3). On the same occasion Peter had voiced that opinion too: 'He [God] made no distinction between us [Jews] and them [Gentiles], cleansing their hearts by faith' (Acts 15:9). James, the leader of the council, concurred: 'It is my judgment that we do not trouble those who are turning to God from among the Gentiles' by imposing the requirement of circumcision on them (Acts 15:19). Faith is enough to bring salvation without adding requirements from the law of Moses or any other code.

In fact, adding requirements can cancel the effectiveness of faith, because for salvation to be by grace, faith must stand alone (cf. Eph. 2:8-9). Otherwise, human merit enters the picture and trust in God is no longer complete. By injecting works into the formula, a person places himself back under the old economy where justification is an impossibility. Paul illustrates the impossibility in Galatians 5:3 when pointing out that every man who is circumcised obligates himself to do the whole law. Doing the whole law is a human impossibility. He continues in Galatians 5:4 by announcing the severance from Christ of all who are trying to be justified by law. That effort on their part separates them from the grace of God.

Elsewhere Paul emphasizes the impossibility of mixing grace and works: 'If it is by grace, it is no longer on the basis of works, otherwise grace is no longer grace' (Rom. 11:6). The moment anyone injects the least element of works into the formula, God's grace ceases to be grace. For Paul to have condoned the inclusion of restricted table fellowship or circumcision among Christians of any background would have meant nullifying the grace of God. He did not want to do that (Gal. 2:21a). Such teaching as includes imputing saving benefits to works implies that righteousness comes through the law. If it does, Christ died in vain (Gal. 2:21b).

Paul's discussion later in the epistle shows clearly that he is not ruling out good works *resulting from* salvation by faith. Freedom from the law does not equate to liberty to practice evil. In Galatians 5:6 he explains that 'in Christ Jesus neither circumcision nor uncircumcision means anything, but faith working through love does.' Though faith and works of the law cannot coexist, faith can produce works. A little later he writes, 'You were called to liberty, brothers, only not liberty as an occasion for the flesh, but through love serve one another' (Gal. 5:13). Relations among the Galatian churches were far from cordial (see Gal. 5:15). Love was sadly lacking among them. The solution was not to enforce legal guidelines to resolve their difficulties. Their need was for faith working through love.

Paul dwells on the role of the Spirit in producing that love when he commands the readers to walk in the Spirit (Gal. 5:16). Then he notes, 'If you are led by the Spirit, you are not under law' (Gal. 5:18). As in Galatians 3:2, reception of the Spirit comes through the hearing of faith, not the works of the law. The leading of the Spirit and the compulsion of the law are contrasting motivations, the latter producing the works of the flesh (Gal. 5:19-21) with their loveless impact and the former producing the fruit of the Spirit whose leading component is love (Gal. 5:22-23).

In magnifying the fruit of the Spirit, Paul injects the death-life paradox once again in Galatians 5:24: 'Now those who belong to Christ Jesus have crucified the flesh with its passions and desires.' In other words, believers have died with Christ in regard to their fleshly passions and desires. In lieu of that lifestyle, they now live in the Spirit as Galatians 5:25 notes: 'If we live by the Spirit, let us also walk by the Spirit.' Since the Spirit of Christ wants to live Christ's life through them, they should allow Him to do so. With Paul they should say, 'Christ lives in me' (Gal. 2:20c).

Two types of motivation

As long as the Mosaic law governed life in Israel, the people subject to it had explicitly stated rules they were to obey. Obedience to those rules did not save them, but faith that demonstrated itself by such obedience did. The laws given by God through Moses were guides that people followed in trying to please God. That written code was an external system that imposed restraints to keep them in paths of righteousness.

Since Christ died, however, that code has been out of date. He ended the law's term of jurisdiction by fulfilling its demands (Rom. 10:4). Believers no longer look to that external restraint for guidance, because since the day of Pentecost they have an inner constraint to guide them. The Holy Spirit supplies guidance in fulfilling the righteous standards that God requires. Walking in the Spirit frees one from the limitations of walking under the law (Gal. 5:18). Walking under the law generates works of the flesh that created such turmoil in Galatia (Gal. 5:19-21). Human depravity responds negatively when motivation for Christian living comes from rules imposed upon it externally. In Romans 7:8 Paul alludes to this characteristic: 'Sin by taking occasion through the commandment accomplished in me every lust.' Only when he began relying on the guidance of the Holy Spirit was he able to live up to God's righteous standards. He states this in Romans 8:3-4: 'What the law could not do in that it was weak through the flesh, God did by sending his own Son in the likeness of sinful flesh and for sin, condemned sin in the flesh, that the righteous requirements of the law might be fulfilled in us, who do not walk according to the flesh but according to the Spirit.'

The Spirit dwelling within Christians provides constraining motives that activate them to godly pursuits. That difference in motivation is the basic difference between the course that Paul was charting for the Galatians and the one proposed by the Judaizers. External restraint causes the flesh to rebel; internal constraint brings compliance with what God expects. The believer's co-crucifixion with Christ releases him from those external restraints that hinder the Spirit's working in his life. His co-resurrection with Christ is essentially the freeing of the Spirit to live Christ's life through him.

Where do the Galatian lessons lead us?
As I was completing this chapter, a couple came to my door with a pamphlet entitled 'Life in a Peaceful New World.' They were representing the Watch Tower Society. A sentence toward the end of that pamphlet said, 'If we truly want to live in God's new world, we must first learn God's will and then do it.' Though they claimed to be believers in Christ, they were advocating good works levied on man by God's law as the means for gaining access to the coming Paradise on earth.

In addition to other doctrinal flaws, theirs was basically the same error as that of the false teachers in Galatia: faith in Christ is necessary, but it is not enough. Forbidding table fellowship with Gentiles in essence teaches that Jewish Christians are partially under law and partially under grace. Advocating circumcision as an additional condition for salvation also says that faith in Christ is not enough. Paul taught that these were impossible combinations. Faith in Christ plus nothing is completely adequate on its own. In fact, it must stand on its own to produce justification and allow for ongoing sanctification. Only faith working through love can move a believer to allow the Holy Spirit to produce the fruit of the Spirit in his life.

The following chart summarizes the discussion above and emphasizes the critical importance of the death-life paradox in Christian self-concept:

The Old Way	The New Way		
	Death: end of the Law's restrictions	**Life** (Christ lives in me): lived by faith in the Son of God	Faith working through love: the solution
The Law's external restraints: limited table fellowship, circumcision, etc.			
	Crucified with Christ: freedom from the Law	Faith: impossible to mix with the works of the Law	Love through a walk in the Spirit: internal constraint

Chapter 3

COUNTERACTING WRONG RULES

Colossians 2:20–3:16

Colossians 2:20–3:16

²⁰If you died with Christ departing from the elementary principles of the world, why as though living in the world, do you submit to decrees: ²¹'Do not handle, do not taste, do not touch' ²²(all things which are destined to perish with the using), according to the commandments and teachings of men? ²³These are matters which have the reputation of wisdom in self-imposed worship and humility and severe treatment of the body, not of any value against the indulgence of the flesh.

¹If then you were raised with Christ, keep seeking the things above, where Christ is seated at the right hand of God. ²Think about the things above, not the things on earth. ³For you died and your life is hidden with Christ in God. ⁴When Christ, who is your life, appears, then you also will appear with Him in glory.

⁵Therefore put to death the members of your body that are on earth, immorality, impurity, passion, evil desire, and greed, which is idolatry, ⁶on account of which things the wrath of God will come, ⁷in which you also once walked when you lived in them. ⁸But now you also, put them all aside: anger, wrath, malice, slander, abusive speech from your mouth. ⁹Stop lying to one another, since you laid aside the old man with his practices, ¹⁰and have put on the new man who is being renewed to knowledge according to the image of the one who created him, ¹¹where there is not Greek and Jew, circumcision and uncircumcision, barbarian, Scythian, slave and freeman, but Christ is all and in all.

¹²Therefore, as those who have been chosen of God, holy and beloved, put on hearts of compassion, kindness, humility, gentleness, patience, ¹³bearing with one another and forgiving each other, if anyone has a complaint against anyone; just as the Lord also forgave you, so also should you. ¹⁴And beyond all these things put on love, which is the bond of completeness. ¹⁵And let the peace of Christ rule in your hearts, to which you were also called in one body; and be thankful. ¹⁶Let the word of Christ dwell in you richly, with all wisdom teaching and admonishing one another with psalms, hymns, spiritual songs, singing with thanks in your hearts to God.

A double heresy in Colosse

False teachers at Colosse were bombarding Christians in that town with a two-pronged heresy. One prong resembled the one being propagated in Galatia, to the effect that Christians were under a continuing obligation to observe the regulations of the Mosaic law. The other prong probably took its cue from a pagan religion that advocated ascetic practices and the worship of angels. Indications of these heresies appear in **Colossians 2:16-19.**

Verse 16 reflects the kind of Judaizing pressure that was afflicting the churches of Galatia. Paul urges the readers of Colossians not to respond to anyone who condemned them because of their dietary habits. Of course, the Mosaic law had strict instructions regarding what the people of Israel could eat and drink (see Lev. 11:4; 20:25; Deut. 14:3, 7). Those regulations no longer applied to believers. He gives the same prohibition against submitting to anyone who condemned their failure to celebrate religious festivals, new moon celebrations of the Jewish calendar, or Sabbaths which Israel regularly observed. Believers were to exercise their Christian liberty and not allow the errorists to undermine it. Such issues were not to become a test of piety or fellowship in the church.

Verse 17 reminds them that those Mosaic restrictions were only shadows of the spiritual reality that eventually came with Christ's death and resurrection. The realities that the law foreshadowed for so long belong to Christ. Once the realities have arrived, no place remains for the shadows, composed of external stipulations, to regulate one's way of life. Christ has released believers from these. Of course, He has not given them liberty to live any way they please. Rather, He has replaced those external restraints with an inner constraint that operates within each Christian through leading of the Holy Spirit.

The other type of insistence from the false teachers incorporated teachings about an infinitely long chain of angels that separated the totally evil world from a totally holy God. These emanations were sufficiently numerous to preserve God's holiness from being polluted by the world of evil. The teaching reasoned that since God was too majestic to be addressed, worship should be directed to these angels that composed this alleged chain. In the second century AD, this type of teaching developed into a well-defined Christian heresy called Gnosticism. It held that Christ was just one link in this long chain connecting with God, and therefore He was not uniquely the Son of God. That is why Paul goes to such great pains in Colossians 1:13-20 to emphasize Christ's uniqueness.

One kind of practical outworking of this heresy was the advocacy of an ascetic lifestyle such as was practiced by the first-century Essene community among the Jews. Abstaining from various types of activities that were allegedly defiling was a part of this false religion. Self-abasement that Paul refers to in Colossians 2:18 and the prohibitions against touching, tasting, and handling in 2:21 related to this view of the world as totally evil. One should avoid any contaminating contact with it.

The two branches of heresy had one thing in common: both consisted of man-made rules that the propagators presented as mandatory for Christians seeking a higher lifestyle. Both promoted as mandatory 'the rudiments of the world' (2:8, 20) that were patterned according to 'the doctrine of men' (2:8; cf. 2:22). Neither gave Christ His rightful place in their schemes. 'Not holding the head' (2:19) means that by worshiping angels, deluded Christians could not give Him first place in their worship the way they should. It also means that by insisting on the permanence of the Mosaic system, they depreciated the merit of Christ's work. In essence, manmade rules had replaced the person and work of Christ in the daily lives of those under the influence of this false teaching.

Motivation to replace manmade rules

Furnished by the death of Christ

The issue in Colosse was not so much what Christians did as why they did it. Their motives for Christian living needed a thorough purging. The erroneous influences at work among them prescribed man-made rules as guides for behavior. Paul insisted that these man-made rules were distorting the truths about Christ and were robbing the Galatian believers of a close relationship with God. Another type of thinking needed to replace compliance with these external regulations as the reason for doing what they did.

He reminded his readers that death had separated them from that kind of living. Because of their union with Christ in His death, they too had died when He died (2:20). Paul asks, 'Why do you act as people living in the world by allowing those elementary rules expounded by the world to be propagated among you?' (2:20). His lesson is, 'Those are rules accepted by people who still belong to this world, but you are not among them. You have been separated from that relationship through death. Somehow others think they can find favor with whatever god they worship by obeying such rules as 'do not touch, do not taste, do not handle' (2:21). Don't allow yourselves to be recaptured by that delusion. That is a man-made motivation.'

All the items from which man-made rules told people to refrain were destined 'for destruction through use' (2:22). God created food and drink to be consumed to sustain human life. Implicit in Paul's words are two objections to the man-made rules. First, they contradict the purpose of divine providence which brought physical sustenance into existence for human use and satisfaction. Second, items that were created to be used up have little connection with genuine piety. Closeness to God does not depend on abstinence from such items. As Jesus said, 'Nothing from outside entering into a person can defile him' (Mark 7:15), and as Paul said elsewhere, 'Food is for the stomach, and the stomach is for food' (1 Cor. 6:12) and 'Everything created by God is good, and nothing is to be rejected, if it is received with gratitude' (1 Tim. 4:4).

External and ceremonial practices do not provide a basis for spirituality. They may be outwardly impressive, but they are of no value in combating fleshly indulgences (Col. 2:23). They cannot accomplish the inner change needed by fallen human beings. That change begins with inward motives and thoughts, and works its way to outward behavior. For Christians the change begins with contemplating death with Christ and resurrection with that same Savior. Believers in Christ should think of themselves paradoxically, which Paul continues to expound in his Colossian message.

Furnished by the resurrection of Christ

The first verse of Colossians 3 turns to the other side of the paradox, the believer's co-resurrection with Christ. That he/she has been raised with Christ is beyond question. Positionally, when Christ came forth from the tomb, so did he/she (Col. 2:12; Rom. 6:4-5, 8, 11). In light of this joint-resurrection with Christ, Paul commands the believer to seek things above, that is, in heaven where Christ currently sits at the right hand of God. Seeking things above eliminates any effort to comply with rudimentary, man-made rules that belong to this worldly realm. Heaven is another sphere of existence where motives spring from inner constraints to please Christ. Changing to that system of motivation frees a person from having to comply with man-made principles that in the long run produce no benefits.

Verse 2 of the third chapter becomes more specific: 'Keep setting your mind on the things that are above, not the things that are on the earth.' Setting one's mind on something speaks of the inner disposition that prompts the practical pursuit of seeking what is spoken of in verse 1. It speaks of the way a person thinks about himself. If he thinks of himself in terms of his co-resurrection with Christ, the inevitable outcome will be a quest for values that relate to heaven, not those that relate to this earth where man-made rules thrive as religious guidelines. The apostle's goal is to get the Colossian readers to act on the basis of motives of inward constraint rather than those that stem from external restraint.

Christ's resurrection life flowing through the believer changes that person's system of values. One who has risen with Christ will look at attachment to things on the earth in a different light, as out of harmony with his new position and outlook for the future. He will not sacrifice all for material possessions because he has treasure laid up in heaven. He will not make honor among men his top priority because of his enthronement in the heavenly places. Earthly pleasures will not be his primary goal because of the newness of life he enjoys. He will not grasp for power because of moral omnipotence that is his for the taking. Fame will not be for him a major achievement since he already has the approval of God. His reason for doing what he does will not be to impress men by obeying a set of rules they have concocted. All these are things related to the earth. The discerning Christian centers his interest on things in heaven.

In Colossians 2:3 Paul reminds his readers once again of their death with Christ (cf. 2:20). Because of that death 'the things that are on the earth' (2:2) should have no appeal for them. He also points out that the life of Christ which is now theirs is hidden with Christ in God. By this he means that it is a life that is spiritual in nature and therefore not visible outwardly. It is a matter of inner experience, but nevertheless a very real life. It is hidden with Christ because their union is with Him in God. Though it is currently invisible, the life is available for present and preliminary enjoyment.

That life will not remain invisible forever, however, because 'When Christ, your life, appears, you also will then appear with Him in glory' (Col. 2:4). Christ is our life as Paul indicates a number of places in several different ways. In Galatians 2:20 he writes, 'Christ lives in me.' In Romans 8:9-10 he adds, 'However, you are not in the flesh but in the Spirit, if indeed the Spirit of God dwells in you. But if anyone does not have the Spirit of Christ, he does not belong to Him. And if Christ is in you, though the body is dead because of sin, yet the Spirit is life because of righteousness.' As our life, He lives in us through His Spirit whom He has sent.

Paul viewed the return of Jesus Christ as imminent. He anticipated the possibility of Christ's coming before his own death (1 Cor. 15:51-52; 1 Thess. 4:15-17). At the time of that appearing our life will no longer be invisible. It will be fully visible as we appear with Him in glory. When that happens, of course, earth will no longer offer any allurements to attract our affections. Man-made rules that fall so far short in leading to a close relationship to God will no longer pose a problem, because our flesh which finds them so attractive in winning the admiration of other men will no longer be a factor in our thinking. Our death and resurrection with Christ will be the only considerations to motivate our decisions.

The death-life paradox and Christian liberty
The Christian's change in motivation from obeying man-made external rules to allowing Christ to live through him is indeed a

liberating transformation. Yet it does not free him from observing principles of love and righteous living. Rather, it frees him to abide by those principles as he is guided by the dictates of an inner compulsion. To guide him in discerning those dictates, in Colossians 3:5-16 a statement of some of the principles follows Paul's strong emphasis on the believer's co-crucifixion and co-resurrection with Christ.

Dispensing with the dead members
Building on the foundational truth of the death-life paradox, Paul first urges his readers to act in harmony with their spiritual union in/with Christ and allow their death with Him to diffuse throughout the members of their old man (Col. 3:5-9). Those are the members that are on the earth. In the words of Romans 8:13, he encourages them by the Spirit to put to death the deeds of the body. Those deeds of impurity include fornication, impurity, passion, evil lust, and covetousness, which the apostle equates with idolatry (Col. 3:5). They also include wrath, anger, malice, slander, abusive speech, and lying (3:8-9). Such actions as these died when Christ died because believers shared in His death through union with Him.

Someone might criticize Paul at this point. At the end of chapter two he strongly forbade compliance with rules imposed by men, such rules as 'do not touch, do not taste, do not handle' (2:21). Compliance with those rules, he said, works against Christian growth. Now, however, he is imposing his own rules, in essence saying, 'Do not commit fornication, and stay away from impurity, passion, evil lust, covetousness, wrath, anger, malice, slander, abusive speech, and lying.' Is he not levying a set of rules for believers to obey just like the set he earlier instructed them to ignore?

The answer is no, of course. A moral difference separates one set of rules from the other. The former set lacks the ethical character of the latter set. A more basic difference between the two, however, lies in the motivation behind compliance with the two sets. Motivation behind the earlier set stems from an effort to find favor with a lesser deity, but motivation behind the second set grows out of a spiritual reality of inner transformation. Death to negative moral values has occurred in connection with Christ's crucifixion, producing a thought pattern that allows compliance to work its way from within the believer. Stated otherwise, the admonition is for the believer to become in his actions what he already is in Christ. He should therefore kill those baser activities that belong to the earthly sphere and that are antagonistic to his higher life in Christ.

Addition of the new members
Death is only half the picture, however. Believers need to replace the old garments with new ones appropriate to their newness of life. These include compassions of mercy, kindness, humility, gentleness, and longsuffering (3:12). They need to bear with and forgive one another in cases where differences arise, and above all to love one another (3:13-14). All this will emerge from within as the Spirit lives the life of Christ through them, producing the peace of Christ in their hearts and thanksgiving toward God (3:15). The major difference between complying with these rules and with the man-made rules already condemned by the writer is the origin of the impulse to obey. Paul makes very clear that the source of the new 'garments' believers are to put on is within themselves as he encourages them to let the word of Christ indwell them richly (3:16).

A system of external compulsion will never work favorably with mankind because of human depravity. Even the Mosaic code that had God as its origin was unsuccessful as the writer to the Hebrews points out. In giving the new covenant, God found fault not with the old covenant but with those to whom that covenant was addressed. Hebrews 8:8 speaks of 'finding fault with them,' that is, the people of Israel. People in general are the reason that external rules will never work. That's why the new covenant provides believers with a new heart that would furnish impetus from within to comply with standards of righteousness. That's why Paul focuses on the heart (3:15) and the indwelling of the word of Christ (3:16). As God's people allow the indwelling Spirit to direct their thoughts, appropriate actions of love and harmony will replace bickering and disharmony.

An important outworking of love

Love as an evidence of the Christ-life in the believer has numerous manifestations, but one is very important to emphasize in connection with Paul's teaching on Christian liberty in the Colossian epistle. Paul has no occasion in Colossians to allude to this Christian responsibility as he does in other epistles. That is the love-generated concern not to cause a Christian brother or sister to stumble.

In 1 Corinthians 8 Paul contrasts love with loveless knowledge. From the standpoint of Christian liberty, he acknowledges that things sacrificed to idols are a non-issue because of the non-reality of false gods represented by those idols. Yet he also recognizes that all men do not have an awareness that this is a non-issue. So in deference to those without this awareness, he urges, 'Take care lest this liberty of yours somehow become a stumbling block to the weak' (1 Cor. 8:9). The path of love is to surrender the use of one's Christian liberty to keep from causing another person to sin.

The apostle deals with a similar issue in Romans 14–15 when he describes a situation in which 'one man has faith that he may eat all things, but he who is weak eats vegetables' (Rom. 14:1). His advice in this situation is, 'Let us not judge one another anymore, but rather determine this—not to put an obstacle or a stumbling block in a brother's way' (14:13). Later he repeats the same lesson: 'It is good not to eat meat or to drink wine, or to do anything by which your brother stumbles' (14:22). He reminds the readers in Rome that Spirit-generated love looks out for the well-being of others: 'We who are strong ought to bear the weaknesses of those without strength and not please ourselves. Let each of us please his neighbor for good, for edification. For even Christ did not please Himself' (15:1-3a). An identifying mark of Christian strength is the concern for others about which Paul speaks here. Such must be the guideline in exercising Christian liberty.

Paul sums up Spirit-led restrictions on Christian liberty well when he writes, 'You were called to liberty, brothers; only not liberty as an occasion for the flesh, but through love serve one another' (Gal. 5:13). In correcting the Colossian error, we must remember Paul's instructions about liberty elsewhere. Liberty allows us to follow the inner-generated impulse to love and show concern for others.

Twenty-first-century Christians face an immense challenge in demonstrating love in this manner. Unfortunately many believers today don't seem to be aware of this channel as an expression of their love for fellow-Christians. Many stumbling blocks are plaguing our current society, for which we need constantly to watch.

(1) The use of tobacco. Many even in the secular society have come to recognize the harmful effects of this habit-forming substance. Yet some professing Christians continue their use of it, thereby influencing others to do the same.

(2) The use of intoxicating beverages. Some Christians see no harm in having a social drink now and then, never stopping to realize their influence on others who may develop into alcoholics as a result of seeing their social drinking.

(3) Attendance at places of entertainment that glorify sinful sex, violence, and God-dishonoring language. Even if Christians can subject themselves to these influences without being affected—which is highly doubtful—love should constrain them to refrain from doing so to avoid causing others to stumble, those who cannot escape the effects of such portrayals.

(4) Participation in lotteries and other forms of gambling. Some Christians feel that slot machines and other 'harmless' forms of gambling are okay as a pastime. Have they stopped to consider how their influence may be the starting point for another who cannot stop with the 'harmless' and will proceed to become a slave to the gambling habit?

(5) Social dancing that excites wrong sexual appetites. Even if some Christians think they can handle these appetites—a doubtful assumption—Spirit-generated love would constrain them to refrain so as to keep from influencing someone else who will stumble when doing the same.

Christians use their liberty to participate in these and other potentially non-edifying activities, because they themselves claim immunity to temptations promoted by such habits and pastimes. That people have stumbled in all these and other areas is beyond dispute. Where is the loving concern for others who may not be immune and fall into sin because of influence from a thoughtless use of Christian liberty? Paul urges, 'Whether, then, you eat or drink or whatever you do, do all to the glory of God. Do not cause either Jews or Greeks or the church of God to stumble' (1 Cor. 10:31-32). God's people need a greater sensitivity to the impact of their lives and actions on others, not just other Christians, but other people regardless of their spiritual status in life.

The net effect of Christian liberty
Christian liberty releases believers from obligations to comply with manmade rules that allegedly bring favor with God. Those represent a system of outward restraint that can never suffice in producing a closer walk with Him. External prescriptions can and usually do generate social turmoil among those striving to comply with them.

Because of their death with Christ at Calvary, believers now enjoy freedom from such externalities, a freedom to respond to the inner promptings of the Spirit of God. They may now think of themselves in terms of the spiritual realities of heaven that free them from degrading and sinful ways and enable them to live on the high plane where Christian love prevails in human relations. That love dictates, among other actions, that believers in exercising their Christian liberty be especially cautious not to cause others to stumble.

Early in my teaching career at one institution, the faculty encountered a small group of students who argued that the school's code of conduct was legalistic and that because of the liberty believers enjoy in Christ, the code should be abolished. They resisted compliance with the rules and wanted freedom to conduct themselves in any way they pleased. In response to this situation, I wrote a brief article in the school publication in which I asked the question, 'Was Paul a Legalist?' I pointed out in the article that complying with rules in itself was not legalism. Legalism consists of complying with rules to earn merit. Paul complied with rules by having Timothy circumcised (Acts 16:3), but he did not do so to earn merit. He did so out of loving concern for others, that is, to keep Timothy from being a stumbling block to Jewish people he sought to serve. Paul submitted himself to the Law's requirements, not to earn merit with God, but to win people to Christ (1 Cor. 9:20). Following rules is not in itself a bad thing. The ultimate issue is one's motives for following rules. In other words, it is not what you do but why you do it that matters with God. If a person follows rules because of loving concern for others generated by the Holy Spirit within that person, that is wholesome Christian conduct. Codes of conduct at Christian institutions are generally intended to encourage loving concern for other people by not setting examples that would cause them to stumble.

The following chart summarizes the discussion above and emphasizes the critical importance of the death-life paradox in Christian self-concept:

The two stages	Different rules to live by	Different places where life is lived	Different motivations	Different outcomes
Stage #1: *before* death and resurrection with Christ	prohibitions against touching, tasting, and handlaing	the old sphere: earth	external: the praise of men	appearance of wisdom, self-made religion, self-abasement, and severe treatment of the body
Stage #2: *after* death and resurrection with Christ	purity, mercy, kindness, humility, gentleness, longsuffering	the new sphere: heaven, where Christ is	internal: constraint by the Spirit	Christian liberty: loving concern for others

Chapter 4

EVALUATING FAMILY TIES

Matthew 10:37-39

Matthew 10:37-39

[37]*The one who loves father or mother more than Me is not worthy of Me; and the one who loves son or daughter more than Me is not worthy of Me.* [38]*And the one who does not take his cross and follow after Me is not worthy of Me.* [39]*The one who finds his life will lose it, and the one who loses his life for My sake will find it.*

Jesus began His ministry shortly after being baptized by John the Baptist. He spent the first months of that ministry in Judea, until opposition from Jewish leaders forced Him to withdraw to Galilee. There He launched a public ministry that lasted fifteen or sixteen months and attracted wide attention.

After reaching Galilee, Jesus called five of His twelve disciples whom He later called apostles. The Gospels do not furnish details for the calling of the other seven, but the five responded to His call at great personal sacrifice. Peter and Andrew left their occupations as fishermen to follow Him (Matt. 4:20; Mark 1:18). James and John left their occupations as fishermen and left their father to follow Him (Matt. 4:22; Mark 1:20). In fact, these four left everything to follow Him (Luke 5:11). Matthew left a lucrative position as a tax collector to follow Jesus (Matt. 9:9; Mark 2:14). Luke summarizes his sacrifice by saying 'he left everything behind' in order to follow Jesus (Luke 5:28).

We may reasonably suppose that these five are typical of the rest of the Twelve whom Jesus sent on a special mission near the end of His lengthy ministry in Galilee. At that point Jesus, being deeply troubled over seeing so many sheep without a shepherd, told His disciples to pray for workers to reach the many people who still needed to hear the good news about the kingdom (Matt. 9:35-38). Then He divided them up into pairs and gave them detailed instructions before sending them out to accelerate the spread of the good news (Matt. 10:1-42).

Family feud (Matt. 10:34-36)
A significant part of those instructions forewarned the Twelve about the persecution they would encounter (Matt. 10:14-23). They could expect nothing different from the opposition that Jesus Himself had already received (10:24-25; see Matt. 12:22-32).

That set the stage for Jesus to tell the Twelve about a looming family feud. In the United States 'Family Feud' is a television program with two families competing against each other by answering questions, but the family feud of which Jesus was to speak pitted members of the same family against each other. Perhaps the most sobering of all were the Lord's instructions about the divisions their message would create, even division of family members against family members. Jesus said, 'Do not suppose that I came to cast peace on the earth; I did not come to cast peace but a sword. For I came to divide a man against his father and a daughter against her mother and a daughter-in-law against her mother-in-law, and a man's enemies will be members of his household' (10:34-36). Already in 10:21-22 Jesus had warned his disciples of family strife. Beginning at verse 34, His words are much more pointed, however.

The words of Matthew 10:35-36 draw from Micah 7:6 as Jesus reflects on earlier divisions resulting from the wickedness plaguing Ahaz's reign over Judah. Those divisions happened as a result of the abundance of wrong values being imposed on the people of Judah. The Micah context pictures a time of strife before eschatological deliverance. Prevailing wrong values caused the divisions of Ahaz's days, but an influx of justice and pure leadership will produce the future divisions of which Jesus speaks. In the former case change from right to wrong caused disruption, but in the latter one, it will be a change from wrong to right. People in rebellion against God will resist the standards that Jesus promotes in trying to bring Israel back to God. That will lead to divisions even within immediate families.

The gospel that Christ brought was inherently a gospel of peace whose goal is to bring men to live peacefully with each other (see Isa. 9:6-7; 11:9; Rom. 12:18). Yet that can only happen when men make their peace with God (see Rom. 5:1). A loyal disciple cannot have peaceful relations in a world that is at odds with God (see Jas. 4:4). People in general are in rebellion against the God who has laid down standards that condemn their sinfulness. They will resent anyone who has chosen to side with God in the great conflict between right and wrong. Friction is inevitable even within the boundaries of one's own family when members are on opposite sides in the battle. That is the division about which Christ speaks. The peace between men that Christ can give is possible only when rebels lay down their arms of rebellion against God. Until then, enemies of God will be enemies of His people and often bitter enemies. That kind of animosity will divide families.

We can wonder whether Zebedee was displeased with the decision of his two sons, James and John, to leave him to carry on his fishing trade alone while they followed Jesus. Running a fishing business alone is not easy. But the cause of the father's resentment may have come even more from his sons' first loyalty being to this stranger rather than to himself.

Quite probably Jesus Himself encountered this kind of opposition from his own brothers (see John 7:3-5). He knew firsthand about family divisions concerning which He spoke to his disciples. His brothers and His mother apparently didn't understand how He could forsake His family to pursue an itinerant preaching vocation (see Mark 3:21). They could not grasp the binding nature of His call, but Jesus could not let that hinder Him. He had to take a stand despite His family's opposition if He was to pursue God's calling. Jesus did so and encouraged His disciples to remain steadfast in pursuing God's call on their lives as He did, even if it meant incurring family opposition. Such a sacrifice was hard, but it was necessary.

About nine months later, during His Later Judean Ministry, Jesus spoke of coming divisions again. That time, just a few months before His crucifixion, He spoke the words to the crowds that assembled to hear His teaching (Luke 12:49-53). On this later occasion He spoke of a father against a son, not just a man against his father (compare Luke 12:53a with Matt. 10:35a); a mother against a daughter, not just a daughter against a mother (compare Luke 12:53b with Matt. 10:35b); a mother-in-law against a daughter-in-law, not just a daughter-in-law against a mother-in-law (compare Luke 12:53c with Matt. 10:35c). So the division works both ways, sometimes a younger generation against an older, and other times an older generation against a younger. Whatever the relationship, the duty of keeping all natural affections subordinate to our love for Christ is supreme (see Matt. 8:22; 19:29; Mark 10:29-30).

Jesus' aim in 10:34-36 was to dispel any superficial notions His disciples might have about what 'peace on earth' (Luke 2:14) means. He brought the sword not to create divisions for divisions' sake, but to reveal the wickedness that lies in the hearts of men.

Choosing a side in the feud (Matt. 10:37)

Jesus continued His instructions in Matthew 10:37: 'The one who loves father or mother more than Me is not worthy of Me; and the one who loves son or daughter more than Me is not worthy of Me.' After describing family divisions and the resulting feud, the Lord presented His listeners with two options: choose your family or choose Me.

A choice to side with Him must be a decisive one. No half-way decision will do. In wording His challenge, He alluded to the degree of dedication Moses expected of the sons of Levi in Exodus 32:26-29 and Deuteronomy 33:9. They had to be willing to oppose any of their own family members who turned their backs on God.

Among Jesus' listeners were men who had already left their past behind to follow Him. Now Jesus tells them that they can expect members of their own families to turn against them. Surely they must have asked themselves, 'Is it worth it? Am I willing to pay that high a price to continue following this Galilean?' Just as such questions may have passed through their minds, Jesus increased expectations even more by comparing their love for father or mother to their love for Himself. At that point His listeners conceivably could have thrown up their hands in despair, thinking that this is a loyalty beyond what could be expected of anyone. How can anyone achieve that kind of dedication?

That meant burning all bridges to the past, even their closest blood ties. Later on, the Lord used even stronger language to emphasize the kind of devotion needed by His followers. During His ministry in and around Perea, within three months before His crucifixion, He spoke of hatred instead of comparative degrees of love: 'If anyone comes to Me and does not hate his own father and mother and wife and children and brothers and sisters, and still even his own life, he cannot be my disciple' (Luke 14:26). Of course, Jesus was speaking hyperbolically in referring to hatred. He did so to emphasize the need for His disciples to love Him more than others. Our love for Him should be so intense that it makes our love for others look like hatred. He certainly did not intend hatred in a nonfigurative sense, because He later ranked love for neighbor as the second greatest commandment (Matt.

22:39) and labeled love for fellow-disciples as a mark of true discipleship (John 13:34-35). His Sermon on the Mount and story of the Good Samaritan taught love even for one's enemies (see Matt. 5:44-45; Luke 10:25-37).

Fortifying one's position in the feud (Matt. 10:38-39)

Family division or feuding is not the ideal case, but in many instances it is reality. It is hard, extremely hard, for Christ's followers to accept. Often their families are the closest people on earth, people they have consistently turned to in times of special need or distress. Now that source of comfort is gone. How can they live with that separation? Can they travel a road that is blocked by that kind of hazard?

To respond to such unspoken questions, Jesus described the frame of mind that would enable His disciples to achieve what He was asking: 'And the one who does not take his cross and follow after Me, is not worthy of Me. The one who finds his life will lose it, and the one who loses his life for My sake will find it' (10:38-39). Jesus' statement recorded in verse 39 is paradoxical because in both parts He uses 'life' in two different senses just as He uses the word 'dead' in two different senses in Matthew 8:22 (i.e., 'Let the [spiritually] dead bury their own [physically] dead'). When He said, 'The one who finds his life will lose it,' 'life' in the first instance refers to earthly, temporal life and 'finds' implies an earnest desire to save that life with its values. That would be the case with a professing disciple who saves his life by recanting his allegiance to Jesus or by keeping quiet when threatened with persecution. The pronoun 'it' stands for 'life,' but life representative of eternal, spiritual life. In the last half of the verse, 'the one who loses his life for My sake will find it,' the term 'life' carries the same two differing meanings. 'Life' stands for earthly, temporal life, and 'it' for eternal, spiritual life. Of key significance in this latter paradox is the necessity of the life being lost *for Jesus' sake*.

Most have heard the saying, 'Finders, keepers, losers, weepers.' Here, however, the tables are reversed: 'Finders, weepers (10:39a), losers, keepers (10:39b).' Of course, the finding must pertain to values of the present life and the losing must be for Jesus' sake for the reversed saying to hold true.

His followers can accept His challenge by viewing themselves as dead in the realm of temporal relations and alive in the new realm of spiritual relations they have formed in Christ. They are now a part of God's family and can turn to their new spiritual relatives for needed encouragement. In other words, they have lost their lives for Christ's sake and gained new lives that are geared to eternal verities.

Worthiness of which Christ speaks equates to worthiness to be His disciple (Luke 14:26) and worthiness to enter the kingdom. To comply with His expectations, His disciples had to adopt a personal value system that viewed themselves as dead to this life's temporal offerings and as alive to the unseen rewards of eternal life. In other words, they had to view themselves as dead in respect to temporal inclinations and alive in respect to eternal verities—a death-life paradox in how they viewed themselves.

In 10:38 Jesus alluded to the death aspect by referring to taking one's cross with the associated loss of life. Death by crucifixion was the means of capital punishment dictated by Roman law. Taking one's cross pictures a criminal bearing his own cross on the way to the place he would be executed, just as Jesus did later on His way to Golgotha. The saying must have seemed strange to the disciples at this point because crucifixion was a Roman custom, not a Jewish one (see John 12:16). Jesus had not yet spoken to them of His coming passion (see Matt. 16:21). Whatever destiny may hold, the Christian disciple is willing to sacrifice everything, even to the point of the loss of life on this earth, for the sake of Christ. Open discipleship exposes oneself to persecution that may lead to martyrdom. That is the level of loyalty expected.

But that is not all. The other side of the self-concept is the high premium placed on spiritual concerns that supersede the values of time. That is what Jesus meant by 'finding' life after losing it for His sake. Following Him is the essence of a life lived in view of the enduring values of eternity. Many years later Paul expressed it this way: 'We do not view the things that are seen, but the things that are not seen; for the things that are seen are temporary, but the things that are not seen are eternal' (2 Cor. 4:18). Such must be the 'self-outlook' of a disciple if he/she wants to follow Jesus without distraction.

Armed with that self-concept, the Twelve to whom Jesus spoke in preparation for their mission throughout Galilee were ready to comply with Jesus' requirement of putting earthly family relationships in a secondary position. If their loyalty to Christ caused their families to turn against them, their choice to love Christ more [i.e., to be loyal or committed to Him more] became a possibility because of their death to temporal relationships. They had a spiritual family to tend to, a family that had come into existence through mutual spiritual ties to Jesus Christ.

Jesus Himself demonstrated that kind of value system when His own flesh and blood became a possible distraction to the ministry He came to implement. They came to Him at a critical point when He was confronting His opponents. They tried to dissuade Him from the course He was pursuing. They even thought He had lost His senses. Rather than acknowledging His family's presence, He pointed out the primacy of His spiritual kin (Matt. 12:46-50; Mark 3:31-35; Luke 8:19-21). Against His family's wishes, He continued to expose the corruption among the leadership of the Jewish nation of His time. That must have been a tough choice for Him, made possible only through His viewing of Himself the same way He was encouraging His disciples to view themselves.

Yet Jesus was not totally oblivious to His family. He fulfilled His duties to His family as His mission permitted. One of His last words on the cross was a provision for His mother's future well-being in committing her to the care of John the Apostle (John 19:26-27). As tradition has it, His father Joseph died while Jesus was still relatively young. Since He was the oldest offspring, Jesus probably became the family breadwinner after that, having learned carpentry from His father (see Mark 6:3). Somewhere around His thirtieth birthday (Luke 3:23), however, He had to launch a ministry in fulfilling His heavenly Father's will (John 4:34). At that point, His family had to realize, as eventually they did, that spiritual priorities must prevail. Jesus exemplified the self-concept that He advocated for His followers.

After receiving Jesus' instructions, His disciples went out

preaching the good news about the kingdom (see Matt. 10:7; 11:1). Presumably they encountered the kind of opposition He told them they would, even from members of their own families. Yet their willingness to discount the importance of earthly ties in order to fulfil an eternal mission fortified them to represent Christ effectively. So effective was their service in Galilee that Herod Antipas, ruler of that territory, for the first time took notice of the impact of Jesus on his domain. Some were saying that John the Baptist whom Herod had beheaded had risen from the dead. Others reported to Herod that Elijah had reappeared, and others that one of the prophets of old had returned. The results of the Twelve's ministry were causes for great perplexity to Herod (see Matt. 14:1-2; Mark 6:14-16; Luke 9:7-9). This multiplied outreach of Jesus' ministry through the Twelve brought Him increased fame and the attention of the ruler of the land. Such can be the impact of any follower of Jesus who is willing to think of Himself as Jesus advocated, as dead in certain regards and alive in others.

Other family feuds
A twenty-first-century disciple of Christ often faces difficult decisions in weighing family loyalties and responsibilities against loyalties to Christ. How does a young person whose parents forbid him to attend church respond? How does a wife whose husband resents her involvement in various avenues of Christian service respond? How does a husband whose wife places lowest priority on the family's responsibility to the corporate testimony of their church in the community respond? How does a pastor whose wife does not support his ministry respond? How does a parent whose effectiveness for Christ is hindered by children in rebellion against God respond?

The response should not be an irresponsible severance of relationship with the family member. That could do more harm than good. Jesus did not cut Himself off completely from His family. The disciple should go out of his/her way to demonstrate the utmost in concern and love for the wayward family member. At the same time, however, the disciple's course of action should be such that it demonstrates a supreme loyalty to Christ and a commitment to what He has called that person to do in this world. The loyal disciple cannot cut himself off from a local body of believers, from witnessing to the lost, from encouraging fellow Christians, and the like. Christ has called all His disciples to those kinds of tasks. To cease doing any of them would be to fail in one's commitment to Him.

At the same time disciples must obey the Lord in such a way that their commitment to Him creates as little antagonism as possible. They must be sure that any animosity that may result from their decision to follow their Master does not arise because of offensive personal conduct on their part. At rock bottom, their motivation should stem from viewing themselves in their early, temporal life as on the way to crucifixion and in their spiritual, eternal being as living for Christ and Him alone.

One's *commitment* to Christ, if it is to be lasting, must be based on a *concept*, a concept of oneself as being dead in the realm where temporal relationships that minimize divine standards prevail, and alive in the realm where eternal relationships that coincide with God's goals are observed.

When I think of this kind of commitment, I think of two brothers, students at the seminary where I teach, who heard God's call to preach and responded with a 'yes.' They had become Christians through the testimony of a church where they lived in the western part of the United States. Their parents, however, were of a Hindu background and strongly resented having their sons receive Christ as Savior. The brothers insisted on attending a church where Christ was honored and the Bible was taught regularly. They became so involved in the ministry of the church that they decided to continue their education in a Christian theological seminary to train for the Christian ministry after they finished college. When their parents heard of this, they decided to cut their two sons off from the family wealth. This came as a considerable shock to the sons, because their parents were quite wealthy and could have provided generous support for them in graduate work and even later. Because of their love for and loyalty to Christ, however, they willingly left the family riches behind. They lost their lives in the earthly, temporal realm, but in so doing, they gained life in the spiritual, eternal realm. Life is now a struggle making ends meet financially, but their lives are rich in the satisfaction of serving Christ by imparting His Word to others. They still cherish their earthly family relationships and meet family responsibilities in whatever ways they can, but for them the importance of those duties takes second place to the importance of serving Christ. Feuding is never enjoyable, but sometimes it is a necessity if one is to follow Christ.

The following chart summarizes the discussion above and emphasizes the critical importance of the death-life paradox in Christian self-concept:

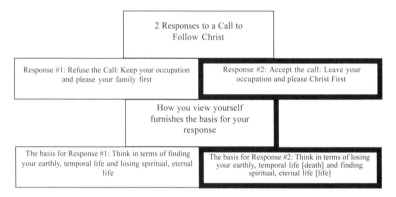

Chapter 5

FOLLOWING CHRIST
IN HIS SUFFERING

Matthew 16:24-26
Mark 8:34-37 Luke 9:23-25

Matthew 16:24-26

[24]*Then Jesus said to His disciples, 'If anyone desires to come after Me, let him deny himself, and take up his cross, and follow Me.* [25]*For whoever desires to save his life will lose it; but whoever loses his life for My sake will find it.* [26]*For what will a man be profited, if he gains the whole world, and forfeits his soul? Or what will a man give in exchange for his soul?'*

About six months after Jesus gave the first recorded 'death-life' instruction to the Twelve, the one recorded in Matthew 10:37-39, another climactic moment came in the life of the group. Jesus had spent most of the intervening time focusing special attention on His closest disciples while limiting His ministry to large crowds that had followed Him much of the period spent in Galilee. During those six months, even when the crowds were present, He seemed to choose actions and words designed to train His closest group of disciples. It was a period of special instruction for them in territories around the fringe of Galilee.

Lessons on Jesus' Messiahship, the church, His coming sufffering

A series of at least six new pieces of information came to light toward the end of that six-month period, when the Twelve were mentally and spiritually prepared to digest them. The series of episodes happened at Caesarea-Philippi while Jesus' group was still outside the territory of Galilee.

(1) The first new fact was Peter's confession of Jesus' Messiahship and deity (Matt. 16:13-17 = Mark 8:27-29 = Luke 9:18-20). Knowing that the time was right, Jesus posed a question to the Twelve, a question as to how these disciples would identify Him. Peter as spokesman for the rest evidenced the conclusion they had reached after witnessing His deeds and listening to His words: 'You are the Christ, the Son of the living God' (Matt. 16:16). Jesus acknowledged the accuracy of Peter's response. Jesus had not until this point directly told them of His Messiahship and deity (though He had earlier made a similar claim to a woman in Samaria [John 4:25-26]). He wanted them to reach a conclusion based on their own observations.

(2) A second new lesson Jesus taught the Twelve at Caesarea-Philippi related to a new work He promised to do, that of building the church (Matt. 16:18-19). This was His first announcement of a new body of people that was to come into being. The initiation and establishment of the church became a necessity when the leaders of Israel evidenced their absolute unwillingness to recognize Jesus as Israel's Messiah by attributing His miracles to Satan (Matt.

12:24-30; Mark 3:22-27). Jesus called their action an unforgivable or eternal sin (Matt. 12:31-32; Mark 3:28-20). Israel's rejection of her Messiah later became even more evident when they participated in His crucifixion. Because the Lord's own people refused His claims, the good news of God's grace has come to the Gentiles, who constitute the large majority of the church, the body of Christ (see Rom. 11:11-12, 19-20, 25). When Jesus first told His disciples about the church, they must have been quite surprised. Their concept of Israel's Messiah was that He would build Israel to international supremacy. His reference to building the church was something their understanding could not assimilate right away. The idea was entirely new to them.

(3) The third new lesson the disciples learned from Jesus on this occasion was the necessity of His coming suffering, rejection, death, and resurrection (Matt. 16:21 = Mark 8:31 = Luke 9:22). This revelation came to the disciples as a shocking surprise. Because of their understanding of Old Testament prophecy, they expected their Messiah to come as a conquering King to reign over the world as His kingdom (e.g., Zech. 9:9). Jesus whom they now had identified as that Messiah was now telling them that He must suffer, be rejected by the elders, chief priests, and scribes, and be killed. Peter's response to Jesus' declaration reflected that this news was too different for the disciples to accept right away. He challenged the accuracy of Jesus' prediction (Matt. 16:22 = Mark 8:32), and in so doing, showed his failure to reckon with another line of Old Testament prophecy that pointed to the sufferings the Messiah must undergo (e.g., Isa. 53:2-10).

It was not until about a year later, after Jesus' crucifixion and resurrection and after the coming of the Holy Spirit at Pentecost, that Peter had a clearer understanding of the need for the Messiah to suffer. In his Pentecostal sermon Peter referred to 'the predetermined plan and foreknowledge of God' that brought the Messiah to the cross (Acts 2:22-23). John the Baptist had the same difficulty as Peter with these two lines of Old Testament prophecy. On the one hand, John prepared the way for Jesus the King to come and rule (Matt. 3:1-12 = Mark 1:2-8 = Luke 3:3-18). On the other hand, he prepared the way for Jesus the Lamb of God who takes away the sin of the world—in other words, the suffering Messiah (John 1:29-34). Though John knew both lines of teaching, even he had difficulty putting the two together. He evidenced his impatience for the coming kingdom when he sent from his prison cell to ask Jesus whether or not He was the coming Messiah (Matt. 11:2-3 = Luke 7:18-20).

Peter came to understand how predictions of both Jesus' suffering and His reign as King could find fulfillment. Jesus' resurrection from the dead, to which Jesus also referred at Caesarea-Philippi (Matt. 16:21 = Mark 8:31 = Luke 9:22), would make possible His future reign as King. As Peter announced so eloquently at Pentecost, His sufferings and death did not end it all. He rose from the grave, allowing Him to return to implement His future reign on the earthly throne of David (Acts 2:24-31).

The lesson on suffering
(4) Peter and the other disciples had a further lesson to learn about suffering, however. That is the fourth bit of news that Jesus had for His disciples at Caesarea-Philippi, and this is where we want to concentrate our attention in the present discussion. He proceeded to tell the disciples and a crowd, whom He had summoned, that to be His disciples they too must be willing to suffer (Matt. 16:24-26 = Mark 8:34-37 = Luke 9:23-25). This second occasion when Jesus taught His followers about the death-life paradox in Christian self-concept came when He voiced principles similar to what He had given the Twelve when He sent them out two-by-two (see Matt. 10:38-39). On this later occasion He elaborated in more detail on how a follower is to view himself: 'If anyone desires to come after Me, let him deny Himself and take up His cross and follow Me. For whoever desires to save his life will lose it; but whoever loses his life for My sake will find it. For what will it profit a man if he gains the whole world but loses his soul; or what will a man give as an exchange for his soul?' (Matt. 16:24-26).

Like Master, like follower
What must Jesus' disciples have thought at this point? Not only was the Messiah talking about His own death, but He was talking about potential martyrdom for His followers. Such was quite remote from the aspirations they had been entertaining for the future. Their

thinking was more along the lines of privileged positions they would occupy in the Messiah's kingdom. In fact, Jesus later promised them they would sit on twelve thrones, judging the twelve tribes of Israel (Matt. 19:28), a prospect that the disciples cherished. Two of them even angered the rest by being the first to ask for the two thrones closest to Jesus' throne in the future kingdom (Matt. 20:20-21, 24 = Mark 10:35-37, 41). These men were thinking future authority, not future suffering and even death. Considerable time had to elapse before they would be ready to accept the role that Jesus was now describing.

Joining Jesus in His itinerant ministry had cost the Twelve dearly. They had left jobs, family, and home to respond to His call. At first, they were not sure what the final outcome of their decision would be, but now they knew Him as the Messiah of Israel, they must realize their honored privilege as members of the inner circle of the one who some day was to rule Israel and the whole world. In twenty-first-century terminology, that must have done wonders for their self-image; their score on the self-worth scale sky-rocketed. But just when they were feeling so good about themselves, along came the news that they must suffer along with their leader. That was a hard pill for them to swallow. It would be a great blow to their self-esteem. How long would it take for them to acquiesce to this totally unexpected role and begin thinking of themselves in terms of the suffering Jesus was promising?

The point finally registered with them, however. Peter was a prime example of those who eventually realized what Jesus meant about the necessity of suffering. About thirty-five years later Peter wrote his first epistle to churches in several areas of what is today northern Turkey. In it he frequently alluded to the possibility of Christians having to suffer. At one point in that epistle he tied that suffering to the suffering and death of Jesus: 'For to this [i.e., suffering for doing good] you were called, because Christ suffered for you, leaving you an example that you should follow in His footsteps' (1 Pet. 2:21). The servant is no different from his Master in this respect. Later in the epistle Peter wrote, 'It is better to suffer for doing good, if the will of God desires, than for going evil. Because Christ also suffered once for all for sins . . .' (1 Pet. 3:17-18). By a later stage in his life, Peter had learned from experience what Jesus was talking about, that the Christian life entails opposition and hardship. The meaning of Jesus' instructions at Caesarea-Philippi finally dawned on him. His understanding didn't crystalize all at once, however. It took time. If extrabiblical tradition is accurate, Peter eventually paid the ultimate price for following Christ by giving his life as a Christian martyr.

Personal desire the starting point for discipleship

To activate the frame of mind Jesus was advocating, He spoke once again about the death-life paradox in Christian self-concept. In this second mention of His call to paradoxical thinking, Jesus elaborated more fully on elements different from what He did in His earlier instructions when commissioning the Twelve. Formerly, He told them, 'Whoever does not take his cross and follow after Me, is not worthy of Me' (Matt. 10:38). Now He expanded to say, 'If anyone wishes to come after Me, let him deny himself, and take up his cross and follow Me' (Matt. 16:24). Several elements in this expanded version deserve special comment. In His Caesarea-Philippi wording the Lord brings in the element of human desire: 'If anyone *wishes* to come after Me.' Wishing is inseparable from how a person thinks of himself/herself. Wishing to follow Christ necessitates conceiving of oneself as first and foremost a follower of Christ. That self-concept stands in direct contrast to an opposite desire Jesus specifies in His next statement: 'Whoever *wishes* to save his life' (Matt. 16:25). In context, that wish is a selfish one because it refers to a self-centered motivation, one that bases values on earthly, temporal satisfaction. That earth-bound self-concept leads inevitably to the loss of eternal, spiritual life. Jesus used the same paradox here that He used on the earlier occasion when He commissioned the Twelve for their mission in Galilee, except here He specified the mental activity behind saving of one's earthly, temporal life. Before He said simply, 'The one who finds his life will lose it' (Matt. 10:39), with no mention of 'wishing.'

Self-denial and cross-bearing based on personal desire

Another addition to His earlier instruction was His positive framing of the guidelines. There He stated in negative terms what would keep a person from being counted worthy: 'The one who does not take his cross and follow Me' (Matt. 10:38). Here His words are a positive command: 'If anyone wishes to come after Me, let him deny himself and take up his cross and follow Me' (Matt. 16:24). He spoke of self-denial, an aggressive first step in implementing the desire to follow Him. More specifically, that first step meant denying what my self claims to be, that is, my master and my king. It is all too natural for people to claim leadership in their own lives, to conceive of themselves as in control of their own actions and destiny. To think of myself as not being the final authority in my own life is radically different, but if my desire to follow Jesus is my prime motivation, I will do that very thing. It all depends on how I think of myself, as a follower of Jesus or as a follower of me.

Just as the Jewish leaders denied Jesus as their King (John 19:15; see Acts 3:13), each follower of Christ must deny himself as ruler of his own life. The nature of Jesus' command (an aorist imperative command in the Greek) calls for an immediate response, not a long, drawn-out process. It allows for no wavering. A person's answer must be either yes or no with no vacillation between the two. If it is yes, it must be a decisive 'yes, I will deny myself.' It can tolerate no hesitation.

The same decisiveness applies to one's response to the next part of His command: 'take up his cross' (another aorist imperative command). From the point of a person's adoption of the self-concept Jesus required, he begins his march toward crucifixion. It is a path leading to suffering and, if need be, death. That was the path that Jesus followed on His way to Calvary; it is the one his disciples must follow. It may not in all cases lead to martyrdom, but the follower must be willing to go that far if called upon to do so. Again, this command is radical, and to comply with it requires that all-out desire to follow Christ.

Following without distraction
Thus far in His instructions Jesus has focused on the 'death' side of the paradox—putting aside the distractions—but when He comes to

the 'follow Me' part, that is where the 'life' comes in. Here Jesus frames His words to speak of a continual process: 'keep on following Me' (a present imperative command in the Greek). This is a life that leads forward into a promising future in time and eternity. To be a learner-disciple, one must follow Jesus constantly, with no lapses or distraction.

Jesus accompanied His command to follow with an explanation that closely resembles the one He gave six months earlier: 'Whoever wishes to save his life will lose it; and whoever loses his life for My sake will find it' (Matt. 16:25; see Matt. 10:39). Instead of using His earlier words 'finding his life,' He now speaks of 'wishing to save his life.' As pointed out above, that wording points more toward how a person conceives of himself, i.e., as a desirer of earthly, temporal prosperity at the expense of spiritual, eternal prosperity.

The positive side of the explanation closely resembles His earlier words: 'whoever loses His life for My sake will find it' (Matt. 16:25) as compared with 'The one who loses his life for My sake will find it' (Matt. 10:39). A further additional detail of Jesus' explanation comes in Mark's account of the Caesarea-Philippi occasion. A person losing his life for Jesus' sake *and for the gospel's sake* is the one who will attain to spiritual, eternal life (Mark 8:35). What one does for Jesus, he does for the gospel, and vice versa. The good news and Jesus are inseparable.

Balancing the books
To clarify the paradox further, Jesus gave His disciples and the assembled crowd one further bit of reasoning: 'What is a man profited if he gains the whole world but loses his [spiritual, eternal] life? Or what will a man give in exchange for his [spiritual, eternal] life?' (Matt. 16:26; see also Mark 8:36-37 and Luke 9:25). Aware that His listeners were thinking His demands to be quite extreme, Jesus used bookkeeping terminology to make His point clearer. How much worldly gain does it take to cancel out the loss of spiritual life? The obvious answer is, it cannot be done. No amount of worldly gain can equal the value of living eternally in the presence of God and His Son. Once lost through a discipleship failure, a person

can never buy back real spiritual life. It is beyond monetary equivalent. Commitment to earthly, temporal values entails the loss of life that is real.

Readers of the gospel accounts of Caesarea-Philippi should recall that Jesus spoke this second lesson about the death-life paradox in the presence of a crowd (see Mark 8:34). The twelve disciples were not the only ones to whom He gave this basic lesson on discipleship. But it was not a lesson on discipleship only, because the Lord spoke of obtaining eternal life. It was a message on salvation too. Is one to conclude that only undistracted followers of Jesus can obtain salvation? Later revelation makes abundantly clear that salvation is by grace through faith in Christ (Eph. 2:8-9), so one dare not make the mistake of basing salvation on works of obedience. Yet the faith that brings salvation inevitably entails loyalty to Christ. Otherwise, it is dead faith (see Jas. 2:14-26). Perhaps the matter is best stated thus: a person with a genuine, active faith in Christ will meet the criteria that Jesus put before the disciples and the crowd at Caesarea-Philippi. That person may waver in his loyalty occasionally. During such a lapse he has room to doubt whether his faith is real, but once he returns to following Christ without distraction, his assurance returns. Those appear to be the parameters Jesus was setting before His listeners at Caesarea-Philippi, a group that included both believers and unbelievers.

Lessons on the coming judgment and on the coming kingdom
Jesus continued on this unusual occasion to give His disciples other new lessons in addition to the four mentioned previously. (5) The fifth was the disclosure of His future coming to judge how people had responded to His lessons on discipleship (Matt. 16:27 = Mark 8:38 = Luke 9:26). The prospects of that future judgment provide powerful motivation for His listeners to adopt the system of values He has advocated in inviting them to become His followers.

(6) The sixth lesson He taught was one of reassurance. He had spoken of His coming death and resurrection. That must have raised a question in the minds of His disciples about the kingdom promised to Israel in the Old Testament. Would His death mean a change in that kingdom program? To assure them that it would not, Jesus promised

that some of His listeners would not die before they saw the coming of that kingdom (Matt. 16:28 = Mark 9:1 = Luke 9:27). A few days later, to fulfill that promise, He took Peter, James, and John up to the top of a mountain and allowed them to witness His transfiguration (Matt. 17:1-8 = Mark 9:2-8 = Luke 9:28-36a). That was a preview of the coming kingdom. It verified that the Old Testament promises of the kingdom for Israel would eventually come to fruition (see 2 Pet. 1:16-19). God will always fulfill His promises.

'All who want to live a godly life in Christ Jesus will be persecuted' is the promise of God's Word. In modern times, many Christians who have lived behind the Iron and Bamboo Curtains can verify the accuracy of that promise. They have suffered physically because of their faith in Christ. Yet physical persecution does not exhaust the ways that enemies of Christ use to afflict God's children. Those of us who have been spared physical pain can vouch for the mental anguish brought on by other types of persecution. Slander, defamation, and denigration that have come our way through non-Christians have hurt us deeply. I remember how those I thought were my friends spoke of my 'going off the deep end' when I began telling others about my new-found faith in Christ. Even professing Christians have been vehicles for inflicting anguish on believers by spreading false rumors about alleged subversive behavior. On one occasion, my pastor informed leaders at the institution where I was employed that I was engaged in undercutting his ministry at my own local church. By conducting myself according to biblical principles, I incurred the deep pain that Jesus promised would come to those who attempt to live godly lives. He promised, 'Blessed are you when people insult you, persecute you and falsely say all kinds of evil against you because of Me. Rejoice and be glad, because great is your reward in heaven, for in the same way they persecuted the prophets who were before you' (Matt. 5:11-12). Persecution includes insults and false accusations, not just physical afflictions. We can accept persecution of any kind as part of losing our earthly, temporal lives, because doing so is part of finding the reward of spiritual life that will never end.

The following chart summarizes the discussion above and emphasizes the critical importance of the death-life paradox in

Christian self-concept:

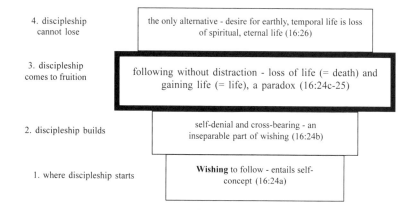

4. discipleship cannot lose

the only alternative - desire for earthly, temporal life is loss of spiritual, eternal life (16:26)

3. discipleship comes to fruition

following without distraction - loss of life (= death) and gaining life (= life), a paradox (16:24c-25)

2. discipleship builds

self-denial and cross-bearing - an inseparable part of wishing (16:24b)

1. where discipleship starts

Wishing to follow - entails self-concept (16:24a)

Chapter 6

EVALUATING
EARTHLY
POSSESSIONS

Luke 14:26-27

Luke 14:26-27

[26]*If anyone comes to Me, and does not hate his own father and mother and wife and children and brothers and sisters, and still even his own life, he cannot be My disciple.* [27]*Whoever does not carry his own cross and come after Me cannot be My disciple.*

The series of enlightening moments at Caesarea-Philippi—the ones discussed in the previous chapter—came in late summer of the year A.D. 29 as Jesus was about to conclude the six-month period of special training for the Twelve. He spent most of those six months in areas outside of Galilee. He followed that period with a three-month ministry in Judea and then another three-month ministry in and around Perea. His third recorded lesson on the death-life paradox came near the beginning of that Perean ministry, some time in the early winter of AD 30.

The lesson on discipleship

This time He delivered the words to large crowds who were following Him. He said, 'If anyone comes to Me and does not hate his own father and mother and wife and children and brothers and sisters, and still even his own life, he cannot be My disciple. Whoever does not bear his own cross and come after Me cannot be My disciple' (Luke 14:26-27). Again, the Lord phrased the paradox in negative terms as He did when He commissioned the Twelve (Matt. 10:38). Again, He used comparative terms that related to one's attachment to various members of his own family, though this time He used the stronger word 'hate' rather than comparing degrees of love (Matt. 10:37). The general force is the same, but 'hate' is a stronger way of speaking about loving less. Again, He spoke of cross-bearing as He did on both former occasions (Matt. 10:38; 16:24). On those other two occasions the words for taking up one's cross are less vivid than in Luke 14:27. Here Luke uses the same word for 'bearing' one's cross that John used when describing how Jesus bore His cross toward Calvary (John 19:17). In contrast to Matthew's account of earlier similar statements, Jesus here uses a tense of the verb that indicates a continuing course of action rather than a crisis, momentary decision. The resultant meaning is that the disciple, having begun, must keep on bearing his cross as Jesus did on the way to Golgotha. Repetition of these points with only slight variations indicates the importance attached to the death-life paradox as a framework for self-concept in Christian discipleship.

Though Luke does not specifically mention the disciples among the listeners in his account of this teaching, they doubtless were present to hear what Jesus told the crowds. The fact that Jesus addressed His teaching primarily to the crowds this time emphasizes that looking at oneself as dead and alive is a lesson for all followers of the Lord, not just the Twelve and not just Christian leaders. This is a frame of mind that needs to be in place for all who consider themselves Christians.

The cost of discipleship

Like a construction project
In teaching the lesson this time, Jesus gave special attention to the price to be paid in becoming His disciple. He used two illustrations to help the crowds understand they should not try to follow Him without thinking matters through beforehand. First, He spoke of an architectural project (Luke 14:28-31). Planning such a project in advance was common practice in those days as it is today. An architect makes sketches of the appearance of a proposed structure. Then structural engineers design the supporting columns and beams necessary to carry the structure. Finally comes the design of the building's outward surface and surrounding landscape. Before any ground is broken, however, various contractors submit bids of their charges if they are selected to do the construction. The owner reviews the estimates and selects the contractor(s) he wants to do the work, unless the amount for construction is more than he can afford to pay. If he has insufficient funds, he cancels the project before breaking ground.

That type of calculation is the proposition that Jesus placed before the crowds whom He had attracted. For the moment, following Jesus was the culturally popular thing to do. The spirit of the hour had swept many into the mood of becoming disciples. Jesus therefore had to take steps to keep people from making frivolous decisions. Becoming His disciple was nothing to be undertaken on the spur of the moment. Such a decision would have serious repercussions in the future.

In warning His listeners of the cost of discipleship, Jesus told about a foolish person who might start to build a tower without calculating the cost of the total project. After laying the foundation, that person would have to suspend further work because of running out of money, making himself the object of ridicule by all parties. A flighty decision to become a disciple would lead inevitably to the same self-imposed penalty of ridicule, when the would-be disciple finds himself unwilling to pay the price of discipleship.

Like planning a military campaign
At the very end of His six-month ministry to the Twelve around Galilee, Jesus had laid down the same stringent requirement for discipleship when He said, 'No one, after putting his hand to the plow and looking back, is fit for the kingdom of God' (Luke 9:62). Realizing the earthly motivations of many in the crowds, Jesus wanted them to know before finalizing their decision that His call to discipleship is not like an invitation to an ice cream social. He therefore proceeded to give them another illustration, this time of a king who anticipates engaging another king in battle (Luke 14:31-32). The potential aggressor will first meet with his strategists to compare his own battle capabilities with those of his intended opponent. In doing so, if he finds his opponent has twice as many troops as his own army, he will doom himself to certain defeat by proceeding with his plans to attack. Were he to go ahead with his aggression without that kind of investigation, he would bring upon himself embarrassment by admitting defeat, surrendering, and asking his opponent for a cease-fire. Losing face in that manner is too unthinkable for a chief of state to risk. He must plan beforehand to avoid that embarrassment. A would-be disciple must do the same.

The desire to follow Christ must be so strong that nothing, not even life itself, is so precious that it will stand in the way of that allegiance. That kind of determination will have its costs. That's why the Lord so often pointed out that a disciple must lose his life for Jesus' sake. That is the 'death' side of the death-life paradox. That is what it means to bear one's own cross as Jesus bore His on the way to crucifixion. Many in the crowds to whom Jesus was speaking apparently had aspirations for the 'life' side of the paradox. They saw the benefits of reigning with the Messiah in His kingdom as something to be sought after. Yet they evidently had not heard what Jesus had told the crowd in Caesarea-Philippi about the necessity of being willing to die for His sake. For that reason, Jesus reiterated that need to these crowds in Perea.

The cost plainly stated

To seal His case and be sure He had made His point, Jesus stated plainly, 'So therefore, anyone of you who will not forsake all his own possessions cannot be My disciple' (Luke 14:33). This point was particularly forceful for the writer Luke, a medical doctor. He returned to it frequently in his writings. He noted that Simon Peter, James, and John 'left everything' in order to follow Jesus (Luke 5:11) and that Levi left everything behind to become His follower (Luke 5:28). He recalled Peter's claim, 'We have left our own homes and followed You' (Luke 18:28) and Jesus' requirement of the rich ruler that he sell all his possessions and distribute the proceeds to the poor if he wanted to become a disciple (Luke 18:22). Luke continued this qualification as a necessity for the ongoing life of the church when he wrote about the earliest believers having all things common (Acts 2:44) and about all things being common property among the earliest Christians (Acts 4:32). He recorded the disastrous results when Ananias and Saphira tried to sidestep this requirement of discipleship by withholding part of their property (Acts 5:1-10) and the exemplary behavior of Barnabas and others in complying with Jesus' principle of forsaking material possessions (Acts 4:34-37). As far as Luke was concerned, the teaching of Jesus about preoccupation with possessions having an ultimately detrimental effect on becoming a disciple was a primary emphasis (Luke 6:24; 8:14; 16:14).

Discipleship likened to salt

To heighten His emphasis on a disciple's willingness to pay the cost of following Him, Jesus introduced a further illustration drawn from various uses of salt: 'Therefore, salt is good, but if the salt also loses its saltiness, with what will it be seasoned? It is useful neither for the ground nor for the manure pile; they throw it out. The one who has ears to hear, let him hear' (Luke 14:34-35). He compared salt's accomplishment of various purposes with that of a disciple in fulfilling his/her role in this world.

The purpose of salt that is obvious to everyone is that of seasoning food to give it a better taste. At the time Jesus spoke the words, most salt in use came from salt beds around the Dead Sea and was mixed with impurities. In other words, pure sodium chloride was unknown. Sodium chloride cannot lose its saltiness, but because of the impurities mixed with it in those days, the sodium chloride could eventually disappear and leave only the impurities. The mixture was no longer useful for seasoning food. Beyond its usefulness in improving the taste of food, salt also was useful when put into the ground as a fertilizer for growing vegetables. Again, salt could function as a regulating agent in controlling the rate of fermentation of a manure pile that was used as a fuel for burning. Without saltiness, however, the substance was no good even for those two secondary purposes.

A disciple in the world is like salt. His presence is an enrichment for the spiritual lives of all people he encounters just as salt enriches the taste of food to which it is applied, that is, as long as the disciple retains his 'saltiness.' In Jesus' illustration the 'salty' disciple is one who has counted the cost of discipleship in advance of deciding to become a disciple. He has determined his own willingness to pay that cost and willingly does so throughout life in bearing his cross and following Christ (Luke 14:27).

Responses to Jesus' standards for discipleship

Undoubtedly, Jesus' requirements for discipleship shocked some of His listeners. The standards He set forth exceeded the upper limits of human imagination. Some in the crowds were saying, 'Impossible! If disciples have to live up to those degrees of self-sacrifice, this man will have no disciples. How can a person hate his own family members and even his own life? If the cost is that great, I will not try to build a tower. If the cost is that great, forget about engaging that other king in battle. If being a disciple costs me all the earthly belongings I have patiently accumulated throughout my life, it is not worth it. I will content myself with contributing nothing to 'flavor' life for others because discipleship costs too much.'

That response to Jesus' lesson on discipleship comes from

people who want to save their earthly, temporal lives. That is the choice they make after weighing the options, particularly the high cost of discipleship. The rich young ruler faced that choice and decided in favor of his riches. Jesus confronted him about this decision by telling him to sell all his possessions and give the proceeds to the poor before becoming a follower (Matt. 19:21 = Mark 10:21 = Luke 18:22). That young man was unwilling to accept the cost of becoming a disciple, so 'his face fell, and he went away grieved' (Mark 10:22).

Many have found some aspects of discipleship attractive when viewing the relationship from a distance, but when brought face to face with the full requirements, they have backed away because, like the rich young ruler, they wanted to save their earthly, temporal life. As their top priority, they may have wanted to salvage family relations, material comforts, or financial security. Something pertaining to this life was more precious to them than following Christ. Jesus' promise to such individuals is the loss of their eternal, spiritual life (Matt. 10:39; 16:25 = Mark 8:35 = Luke 9:24). Their 'this life only' orientation proved to be their demise.

How great it would be if everyone accepted Jesus' invitation to become a disciple! Yet this will not happen. The Bible makes that very plain. Only a few will be willing to lose their lives for Jesus' sake, such persons as Peter and others who had left their homes and everything to follow Jesus (Matt. 19:27 = Mark 10:28 = Luke 18:28). To people like this, Jesus' promises abounded with benefits:

> Everyone who has left houses or brothers or sisters or father or mother or children or farms for My name's sake, shall receive many times as much, and shall inherit eternal life (Matt. 19:29).

> There is no one who has left house or brothers or sisters or mother or father or children or farms, for My sake and for the gospel's sake, but that he shall receive a hundred times as much now in the present age, houses and brothers and sisters and mothers and children and farms, along with persecutions; and in the age to come eternal life (Mark 10:29b-30).

> There is no one who has left house or wife or brothers or parents or children, for the sake of the kingdom of God who shall not receive

many times as much at this time and in the age to come, eternal life (Luke 18:29b-30).

God rewards single-mindedness that centers on eternity's priorities. In this life that reward often comes in unexpected ways as He replaces that from which a disciple has turned in order to follow Jesus, but His reward in the age to come is pre-announced— eternal life.

Faith, discipleship and self-concept

From our post-Calvary perspective we might surmise that Jesus taught that people attain eternal life through meeting His demanding standards for discipleship. John 3:16 offers a refinement to that perspective, however, for there Jesus said, 'For God so loved the world that He gave His one and only Son, that whoever believes in Him should not perish but have eternal life.' A person receives eternal life by faith through accepting God's gift through His Son (see Rom. 6:23). Through His teaching in Luke 14:25-35 the Lord presented the other side of that truth, that one whose faith in Christ is complete and genuine also surrenders willingly to Christ's demanding call to discipleship. Complete dependence on Christ for salvation leads inevitably to obedience to His will. That obedience may experience temporary lapses, but in the long range it will be conspicuous.

A cause for lapse in obedience is usually a person's viewing himself wrongly. He may think more highly of himself than he ought to think (contrast Rom. 12:3), or he may view himself wrongly in other ways. Any one of the wrong views of self is enough to cause him to think of Christ's requirements for discipleship as too tough. The cost is too high. That person's problem is a misguided self-concept, a failure to think of himself as dead in respect to this world's allurements and alive in respect to the values of the age to come. That is the death-life paradox in self-concept that Jesus advocated, without which it is impossible to meet His demands for discipleship. A total commitment to following Him can come only on the basis of a right concept of oneself.

In the terminology of Luke 14:27, a disciple must keep on bearing his cross on his way to death, however and whenever that death may come, and keep on following Christ with all the fruits of life that such a course promises. Following Christ is first of all a person's volitional, mental state before it can work its way out in his/her actions.

One of the rewarding aspects of teaching in a Christian institution that prepares men for vocational Christian service is seeing demonstrated in the lives of students the kind of pre-planning and dedication that Jesus speaks of in Luke 14. I think of a former electronics specialist who left a lucrative career in business to train for ministry, who has now left family connections and friends behind and is now giving his life to teach and help train pastors in another part of the world. I think of a medical doctor who left a promising career in medicine to come to the United States to study so that he could return to his own country to plant a church and start a training institute in his own city. I think of a lawyer with a large family who left a legal career to learn Scripture better so as to prepare himself to train future ministers of the gospel in this country. Many other such examples crowd my mind, men who counted the cost of discipleship and decided it was worth the price they would pay. Not one of them regrets his decision to follow Christ. They all are now basking in the joys of the spiritual life they have received in exchange for the abundant temporal possessions they left behind.

The following chart summarizes the discussion above and emphasizes the critical importance of the death-life paradox in Christian self-concept:

Pre-planning for Discipleship

The Illustrations	Life's Values	Self-Concept	Faith in Christ
1. cost to build a tower too great	1. tasteless salt - family, possessions too precious	1. continuous cross-bearing and following Christ refused in favor of this life's values	1. a superficial faith leading to non-loyalty
2. cost to build a tower worth the investment	2. salt with taste - an enrichment for the lives of others is what counts	2. continuous cross-bearing (**death**) and following Christ (**life**) accepted	2. a genuine faith leading to unswerving loyalty
1. enemy too strong to compete with	1. tasteless salt - family, possessions too precious	1. continuous cross-bearing and following Christ refused in favor of this life's values	1. a superficial faith leading to non-loyalty
2. determination to overcome the enemy's stiff opposition	2. salt with taste - an enrichment for the lives of others is what counts	2. continuous cross-bearing (**death**) and following Christ (**life**) accepted	2. a genuine faith leading to unswerving loyalty

Chapter 7

RESPONDING TO THIS WORLD'S ALLUREMENTS

Luke 17:32-33

Luke 17:32-33

[32]*Remember Lot's wife.* [33]*Whoever seeks to possess his life shall lose it, and whoever loses it shall preserve it alive.*

Jesus spoke often about the kingdom of God. Many times He did so in connection with promises of His second coming to earth. One of those times was near the end of His ministry in and around Perea, just days before His Triumphal Entry into Jerusalem and the beginning of the last week before His crucifixion. That was the occasion of His fourth and next-to-last recorded reference to the death-life paradox in Christian self-concept.

The Pharisees had just asked Jesus about the time when the kingdom of God would come (Luke 17:20). Jesus responded, 'The kingdom of God is in your midst' (Luke 17:21). By this He meant that the kingdom was present with the Pharisees because the King Himself was present among them. After that remark to the Pharisees, Jesus offered His disciples a series of teachings about His return (Luke 17:22-37). During the future period of His absence, He predicted that they would earnestly desire to see the time of His return, but would be disappointed (17:22). He warned against 'false alarms'—that is, people claiming that He had already returned (17:23)—and promised that when He does come back, the event will be so conspicuous it will escape no one's notice (17:24). His second coming could not occur, however, until His suffering and death at the hands of His Jewish opponents (17:25).

The suddenness and unexpectedness of the second advent will be comparable to the suddenness and unexpectedness of the flood in Noah's day (17:26). Life was taking its routine course, including such activities as regular meals and marriage ceremonies, until Noah entered the ark. Then the flood waters put an abrupt end to those routine activities and destroyed Noah's God-rejecting contemporaries (17:27-28; see Gen. 7:6-23).

The second advent will also resemble the surprise judgment on Lot's contemporaries. People in Sodom were engaging in their regular eating habits, commercial habits, farming habits, and construction habits until the day Lot left the city. Then fire and brimstone rained on the city and destroyed all its inhabitants (Luke17:29). Jesus' return will bring the same type of surprise ending for ungodly mankind (17:30).

The error of Lot's wife and its penalty

The Lord followed up illustrations from Noah and Lot with a warning against people becoming so attached to materialistic values that they try to retain their worldly goods at the time of His return (17:31). In other words, they should not make the same mistake as Lot's wife made (17:32). The angels who delivered Lot and his family from Sodom had commanded them to flee and not to look back as they were fleeing (Gen. 19:17). Probably remembering some of the physical comforts she had enjoyed in Sodom, however, Lot's wife did look back at the city as it fell under God's judgment. When given an opportunity, Lot had chosen the valley of the Jordan River where Sodom and Gomorrah lay, because it offered the greatest promise of physical prosperity for him and his family (Gen. 13:10-11). His wife had apparently become quite attached to that prosperous lifestyle, so much so that she directly disobeyed the angel's command. When she looked back, she apparently had some thought of returning to the about-to-be judged city to retrieve some more of her belongings (see Luke 17:31). Because of her disobedience she too became an object of God's judgment and was turned into a pillar of salt (Gen. 19:26). Her error serves as a warning against becoming so attached to this world's comforts that one is unwilling to leave them to join Christ at His coming. In Jewish literature Lot's wife illustrated the behavior of an unbeliever.

The Lord used the love of Lot's wife for Sodom to illustrate the love a would-be disciple may have for this present world and its materialistic pleasures. Anyone who seeks to retain that kind of life will lose the life that is real (Luke 17:33a), He said. Just as Lot's wife forfeited her deliverance from the judgment of God, so will a person forfeit the privilege of spiritual, eternal life by valuing this earth's temporal privileges above privileges that transcend the limitations of time. By following that system of temporary values, a person demonstrates that his faith in Jesus Christ for salvation is not vital, nor is it life-changing. If it were a saving faith, he would view the things of eternity differently from the things of time.

Then Jesus repeated His death-life-paradox principle: 'Whoever keeps his life for himself will lose it, and whoever loses his life will preserve it alive' (Luke 17:33). A person can escape the judgment of God by learning from the wrongdoing of Lot's wife. This time, His wording closely resembled that in Matthew 10:39 and 16:25, but His terms for 'keeping his life for himself' and 'preserving it alive' are stronger than the 'finding' and 'saving' He used on those earlier occasions. 'Keeping . . . alive for himself' is a word that vividly depicts personal ownership, and the two parts of the word translated 'preserving . . . alive' mean 'becoming alive.' The last part of the statement thus places a double emphasis on life: 'preserving life alive.' By thinking of himself in light of that kind of value system, i.e., losing his life in order to 'preserve life alive,' one can escape the clutches of materialism and avoid being penalized when Christ returns. Jesus utilized the death-life paradox once again, this time to prescribe how to avoid God's punishment.

Warnings against the enticements of riches
John the Baptist warned his listeners about attachment to the things of this world. He told the tax collectors who wanted to be baptized not to collect more taxes than they were authorized to collect (Luke 3:12-13). Tax collectors were notorious for padding their own bank accounts by collecting excessive taxes. In answer to their questions, John told soldiers to be content with their wages and not to take money from people by force (Luke 3:14).

Jesus too issued warnings about placing a premium on material prestige, possessions, and comforts.

- He told the Sadducees not to pad their treasures by profit from their money-changing and selling of animals in the Jerusalem temple (John 2:14-16). The Father's house was never intended to be a house of merchandise.

- He warned against laying up for oneself treasures on earth, noting that where one's treasure is, his heart will be also (Matt. 6:19-21).

- He urged the seeking of God's kingdom and righteousness as the first priority (Matt. 6:33).

- He told a parable about how some people's systems of values—including the deceitfulness of riches, the desire for other things, and pleasures—can keep them from responding to the message about His kingdom (Matt. 13:22; Mark 4:19; Luke 8:14).

- He sent the Twelve to preach the gospel of the kingdom, expressly forbidding them to take money with them (Matt. 10:9; Mark 6:8; Luke 9:3). Preaching the gospel is not a money-making business.

- He expressly scolded the 5,000 for pursuing Him just to gain food for their stomachs (John 6:26-27).

- He reprimanded the disciples for thinking in terms of food for the body when He spoke of the leaven of the Pharisees, Sadducees, and Herodians (Matt. 16:8-9; Mark 8:17).

- He also rebuked them for arguing among themselves over who was the greatest according to this world's standards (Mark 9:34-37; Luke 9:46-48).

- He told a parable to a crowd about a certain rich fool, whose crops were extremely productive and who said to himself, 'Soul, you have many goods laid up for many years to come; take your ease, eat, drink and be merry' (Luke 12:16-20).

- He drew from that parable the lesson of what a fool anyone is who lays up treasures on earth and is not rich toward God (Luke 12:21).

- In a Pharisee's home, He gave a parable to the guests about occupying the lowest place rather than the place of honor (Luke 14:7-11).

- He scolded the Pharisees because of their love for money (Luke 16:14-15).

- He contrasted the eternal misery of a certain rich man with the eternal bliss of a poor man named Lazarus (Luke 16:19-31).

- He required the rich young ruler to give away his wealth in order to become His disciple (Matt. 19:21; Mark 10:21; Luke 18:22).

- He delivered the important teaching on servanthood when a dispute arose among His disciples about which two would have the prestige of sitting on His right and left hands in the kingdom (Matt. 20:25-28; Mark 10:42-45).

- A second time He rebuked those who were using the Jerusalem temple for temporal gain (Matt. 21:12-13; Mark 11:15-18; Luke 19:45-48).

- He again had to resolve a dispute among His disciples over worldly greatness (Luke 22:24-27).

Jesus consistently emphasized the need for a disciple to be detached from concerns about what this world considers success, whether it be position, wealth, or comforts. Materialistic concerns constitute an epidemic that has infected most people in the western world at the beginning of the twenty-first century. The first group that comes to mind are the wealthy. Many of them have gained riches and have multiplied holdings as their main goal in life. They cling to their wealth like the rich young ruler did to his. Their attachment to material possessions is obvious.

But another group is just as culpable. Those are people who have few of this world's goods but whose longing for wealth consumes their lives. They think that a quick acquisition of wealth would end all of their problems. Jesus had words for this group too. He told them to seek first God's kingdom and to allow God to meet their daily needs just as He cares for the flowers and the birds (Matt. 6:25-34). The inclination to value earthly gains above all else is almost universal among us, but Jesus taught that we must replace that value system if we want to follow Him.

Self-concept and the return of Christ

Jesus spoke the words of Luke 17:22-37 just days before the final week of His life on earth.Anticipating His crucifixion and resurrection, He looked beyond them to His return and the establishing of His kingdom on earth and saw the need to emphasize once again how a person should view himself. His restatement of the death-life paradox in this setting takes on a greater urgency than heretofore, because a failure to have the right perspective on self will issue in a sad result similar to what befell the contemporaries of Noah and Lot and what Lot's wife reaped. Jesus' words are even more grave in a context with heavy emphasis on the judgment that will occur at His return.

He follows His restatement of the paradoxical principle with a warning of the suddenness of His coming. One of the two people in a bed will be taken from the scene of judgment and the other left to face the judgment (Luke 17:34). One of two people grinding together will be taken away from the scene of judgment and the other left (Luke 17:35). The people taken are those rescued in the same way as Noah and Lot. The people left are those remaining to be judged in the same way as Noah's and Lot's contemporaries. By strong implication, the latter are the ones who seek to keep their temporal lives and lose their spiritual lives. The people taken to safety are the ones who lose their earthly lives for Christ's sake and preserve their eternal life. They will refrain from looking back the way Lot's wife did.

Detachment from the world

Freeing oneself from the world's allurements is no easy task. To some extent every person has to live in this world and adapt to his surroundings. We cannot control everything that comes into our lives. That means that often we will find ourselves confronted with difficult choices, choices pertaining to employment, home location, investment opportunities, recreation outlets, and vast numbers of other involvements in life on earth. At what point do we detach ourselves from all such connections by losing our lives for Jesus' sake? That, of course, must be an individual choice. The important issue lies in how we value all such involvements in relation to how we view eternal values. Whenever our earthly activities cease to be a means of accomplishing eternal goals, we have lost sight of the proper guideline Jesus laid down.

The New Testament is specific in directing Christians away from the allurements that enticed Lot's wife. 'Stop loving the world or the things in the world' (1 John 2:15a), John wrote to believers in the area of the seven churches shortly before Christ addressed seven messages to those churches in Revelation 2–3. John even went so far as to say that a person who loves the world knows nothing of the love of the Father (1 John 2:15b). Under the heading of things in the world he included the lusts of the flesh, the lusts of the eyes, and the pride of life (1 John 2:16). The lusts of the eyes was the main aspect of the world's appeal that attracted Lot's wife, with perhaps elements of the other two appeals sprinkled in.

Paul lamented the loss of Demas' companionship and support. He specified why Demas had deserted him, in 2 Timothy 4:10. It was because he loved the present age. He distorted his sense of values and allowed the things of time to take priority over the things of eternity. Something on his agenda of activities, some pleasure or indulgence, was more important to him than the service he was rendering to Paul in his imprisonment, so he left Paul alone in his dungeon prison-cell. That is the kind of deception that worldly allurements can produce in the lives of those who are otherwise well-intentioned people.

Paul wrote Timothy earlier, 'Charge those who are rich in this age not to be conceited or hope in the uncertainty of riches' (1 Tim. 6:17a). He warned the rich not to become attached to their riches as their top item for attention. Riches are no basis for conceit because they may be here today and gone tomorrow. At best they will only endure till the end of one's life on earth. In light of that limitation Christians should rest their hope 'on God who provides . . . all things richly for enjoyment' (1 Tim. 6:17b). The enjoyment God provides never ends; time places no limitation on it. That enjoyment pays dividends in this life and beyond, into eternity. This world can make no such offer.

Christ gave Himself for our sins 'that He might deliver us from the present evil age' (Gal. 1:4). If Christ has delivered us from the present evil age, how can we allow ourselves to be drawn back into its clutches? How can we longingly look back at Sodom and give even a second thought to wanting to return? How can we allow the glitter and attraction of what this world offers to turn our minds aside from the blessed hope and appearing of glory of our great God and Savior, Christ Jesus (see Tit. 2:13)? Yet some people who claim to be followers of Christ make such mistakes.

Do not underestimate the power of the world. Only by thinking of oneself as dead in that realm—losing one's life for Christ's sake—and alive in the realm of spiritual verities—preserving one's life (Luke 17:33b)—can someone escape the world's enticements permanently. Only then can a person live with a proper anticipation of Christ's imminent return and thereby be ready for Him and His future kingdom. Everyone of us must adopt the correct self-concept, the biblical, Christian way of thinking of ourselves, as Christ so frequently admonished His followers and the crowds.

While he was living, I had the privilege of being an acquaintance of Dewey Lockman, founder of the Lockman Foundation which produced the New American Standard Bible. Dewey became a wealthy man through citrus farming and real estate procurement in the 1930s and 1940s. He actively sought to reach servicemen for Christ through centers he established in southern California during World War II. When he came to the time of deciding what to do with his wealth, he displayed no interest in using it for pleasure, entertainment, fine clothes, expensive automobiles, or any other enticement that this world has to offer. Rather he decided to invest in eternity by placing one-hundred percent of his fortune into a nonprofit foundation dedicated to producing Christian literature and translations of the Bible. He and his wife lived on very limited salaries from the foundation he established. Their sole interest was in following Christ, with nothing of worldly allurements to distract them. Dewey lost his life for Christ and thereby preserved it alive (see Luke 17:33). He avoided the fate of the contemporaries of Noah and Lot and that of Lot's wife.

The following chart summarizes the discussion above and emphasizes the critical importance of the death-life paradox in Christian self-concept:

TWO DESTINIES AT THE RETURN OF CHRIST		
1. now: Lot's wife: looking back	the decisive difference	2. now: detachment from the world
1. now: materialism, love for money	losing life (death) in order to preserve it alive (life), a paradox	2. now: ignoring this life's values
1. reward: judgment, fire and brimstone		2. reward: life in its richest sense

Chapter 8

FRUIT-BEARING FOR GOD

John 12:24-26

John 12:24-26

[24]Truly, truly, I say to you, unless a grain of wheat falls to the ground and dies, it remains alone; but if it dies, it bears much fruit. [25]The one who loves his life loses it; and the one who hates his life in this world will keep it to life eternal. [26]If anyone serves Me, let him follow Me; and where I am, there My servant will be also; if anyone serves Me, the Father will honor him.'

The fifth and last recorded occasion when Jesus spoke about the death-life paradox came on the Monday before the Friday of His crucifixion. Earlier that Monday the Lord had cursed the barren fig tree (Matt. 21:18-19a = Mark 11:12-14) and cleansed the temple a second time (Matt. 21:12-13 = Mark 11:15-18 = Luke 19:45-48). Surprisingly, the request of some people of Greek descent to see Him prompted the teaching this time (John 12:20-21). Philip, one of the Twelve, was the one whom the Greeks approached, and he brought their request to Andrew's attention (John 12:22a).

The request of some Greeks: 'We want to see Jesus'
The two disciples were probably hesitant in approaching Jesus. That Gentiles had expressed interest in Jesus at the beginning of His life is true according to Matthew 2:1-12, but He pointedly limited His first-advent ministry to those of Jewish lineage, telling the Syrophoenician woman that He was sent only to the lost sheep of the house of Israel (Matt. 15:24). He instructed the Twelve along the same lines in forbidding them to go to the Gentiles and Samaritans (Matt. 10:5). He did prophesy about a future ministry to 'other sheep I have which are not of this fold' (John 10:16)—i.e., Gentiles—and before His ascension He was to tell His disciples to go to all nations (Matt. 28:16-20; Acts 1:8). At this point near the end of His life, however, the approach of some Greeks must have put Philip and Andrew in an awkward situation.

They decided to proceed, however, and deliver the Greeks' request for an audience to Jesus. They may have felt the time was ripe for the glory of His prophesied kingdom to become a reality. At the triumphal entry the day before, the Jewish crowds had proclaimed Him King. Up to this moment, the Romans had evidenced no visible opposition. The Greeks were seeking Him. Maybe the time for the kingdom had come, they may have thought.

Jesus' response to the request: 'The time is not right'
Jesus did not respond as Philip and Andrew had perhaps hoped He would, i.e., with an announcement that His kingdom on earth would become an immediate reality. In fact, He did not respond at all to the request of the Greeks. Instead, He spoke of the arrival of the

time for His glorification (John 12:23). In connection with that glorification He continued with an illustration—an obvious reference to His coming death—to point out the necessity for a seed to be planted and die if it is to bear fruit (John 12:24). From that illustration He derived a principle: 'The one who loves his life loses it, and the one who hates his life in this world will protect it for life eternal' (John 12:25). The next verse clearly indicates His application of the principle to His disciples as well as to Himself. It speaks of serving and following Him, remaining with Him, and receiving honor from the Father (John 12:26).

We can rest assured that Jesus gave the death-life principle to Andrew and Philip, but probably the crowd standing nearby heard it too. They heard the thunderous sound of the Father's words, 'I have both glorified it and will glorify it again,' that came immediately after Jesus' statement of the principle (12:28-29). Presumably they also heard what He said just before that.

Jesus' failure to respond directly to the Greeks' request raises the question, 'Why?' Here were people seeking Him. Why did He not welcome them in accordance with His earlier statements, 'Come to Me, all who are weary and heavy-laden, and I will give you rest' (Matt. 11:28) and 'The one who comes to Me I will never cast out' (John 6:27)? The answer to such a question must be the timing of the request; it was premature. Not until after Jesus' death, resurrection, and ascension could the good news go to Gentiles directly. The Lord could not satisfy the desire of the Greeks for a direct audience until He had gone through the unspeakable agony of death. The profound impression on Him brought by this occasion is evident. It awakened in Him a feeling of His relation to the whole world, a direct relationship that would not become a reality until His glorification. Of course, His glorification could come only after His death. That is why He responded the way He did, referring first to the arrival of the hour of His glorification (John 12:23) and then to His death by way of a figurative reference to its necessity (John 12:24).

In effect, Jesus' answer to Philip and Andrew was an indirect response. In essence, He said, 'These Greeks cannot see Me now. A day will come when Gentiles will have direct access to Me, but it will be only after and as a result of My going down into death as a seed goes into the ground and dies. I will emerge from death and be glorified. Then their desire to see Me will be satisfied.'

The universal principle: The necessity of death before life

Jesus' disciples had dreams of Jesus sitting on the throne of a glorious kingdom with themselves ruling beside Him (Matt. 20:21, 24 = Mark 10:37, 41; Luke 19:11; Acts 1:6). With one stroke, however, Jesus temporarily dispelled those dreams. He pointed out the painful necessity of His own death before their dreams could become reality. Jesus Himself did not relish the thought of His coming death. In the incomprehensible make-up of His Godhood-Manhood, He struggled with the agony He was about to face (John 12:27). Earlier the devil had offered Him a route to kingdom glory without suffering, but Jesus had resolutely rejected that route (Matt. 4:8-10; Luke 4:5-8). The time had now arrived for Him to experience not only the physical anguish of crucifixion, but also the spiritual agony of separation from His Father in bearing the penalty for the world's sins (Matt. 27:46; Mark 15:34).

He chose to illustrate the necessity of His death by recourse to the law of increase from the realm of nature. In other words, the law of the seed is the law of life. For a seed to be productive, someone must put it into the ground, allow it to rot, decay, and die if he wants it to bear fruit and produce a crop. As the Lord indicates in John 12:24, that law applies in the human realm. He Himself is that grain of wheat. Had He not died, salvation and forgiveness of sins could never have come to even one poor sinner. His death had to occur before He could be the source of spiritual life for the world. To state it another way, that was the only way He could become fruitful. The phenomenon is paradoxical, but inherent in His death was the potential for life to all men.

As He wrestled with anticipation of the event, He acknowledged that this was His purpose for entering the world at His incarnation: 'Now My soul is troubled. And what shall I say? "Father, save Me from this hour?" But because of this I came to this hour' (John 12:27). He came to engage in the determinative conflict with sin and death. In so doing, He also exemplified a principle that is true of all life. He said, 'If I am lifted up [in crucifixion], I will draw all people to Myself' (John 12:32). The principle He illustrated is that death brings about fruitfulness and without death no fruitfulness can result. His fruitfulness was life, not only His own life after His resurrection but also the life He imparted to those who through faith avail themselves of the eternal life He offers.

The universal principle extended: The death-life paradox
From the illustration in John 12:24 Jesus moved to reality in John 12:25: 'The one who loves his life loses it, and the one who hates his life in this world will protect it to life eternal.' The first half of that statement speaks of the one who refuses to part with the values of earthly, temporal life. For that person spiritual, eternal life is not available. Such a person is a seed that refuses to die and because of his refusal has no access to real life, life that is unseen and eternal. The last half of the verse depicts a person who hates his earthly, temporal life in this world or, in other words, dies with reference to values that are material and visible. This one guards his spiritual life all the way to life eternal.

In a sense, Jesus was still speaking of Himself and applying the illustration of the seed to His own experience. He had to turn His back on values that loom largest in the minds of most human beings. Otherwise, He could not have died and been raised from the dead to enjoy never-ending life. Nor could He have borne the fruit that has been so evident as a result of His death and resurrection. In another sense, however, He laid down the same guideline for His followers, as the next verse goes on to stipulate: 'If anyone serves Me, let Him follow Me' (John 12:26a). This death-life paradox is the same lesson recorded by the Gospel writers on four earlier occasions. On one of those occasions, the one in Caesarea-Philippi (Matt. 16:24-26 = Mark 8:34-27 = Luke 9:23-25), Jesus compared the willingness of His disciples to suffer to His own willingness to do the same. He is doing essentially the same thing here.

The words of John 12:25 serve as a warning to Philip and Andrew. However, the 'hosannas' from the Triumphal Entry of Christ into Jerusalem the day before (Matt. 21:9; Mark 11:9; John 12:13) were still ringing in their ears, possibly leading them to think the days of opposition were past. In just a few days cries of 'Crucify Him' (Mark 15:13-14; John 19:6, 15) were to replace the 'hosannas'. Philip and Andrew needed to prepare for the fickleness of the crowd so as to be ready for the radical mood swing between Monday and Friday of the same week. They needed to cease counting their own lives dear and to view themselves as seed to be put into the ground to rot and decay. Just as Jesus, they needed to pass through self-forgetting sacrifice if they wanted to reap harvests of gracious magnitudes. They needed to be braced to withstand selfishness and cowardice if they wanted the same fruitfulness as their Lord.

They could not, of course, die for the sins of mankind as Jesus did. He and He alone was the spotless Lamb of God who takes away the sin of the world (John 1:29). No one can come to the Father except through Him (John 14:6b; Acts 4:12). He is the only propitiation for the sins of mankind (1 John 2:2). Yet His followers can imitate His self-abnegation by being willing to bear shame for His sake. For them too, selfishness is the destruction of life just as sacrifice and self-surrender are conditions of the highest life. The disciple who would be fruitful must bury his love for the world with its riches, honors, pleasures, and rewards (1 John 2:15).

Wheat may be put to two uses: it may be eaten or it may be sown. A person may chose to eat it and enjoy the momentary gratification and benefit from doing so. Or he may put it into the ground, burying it out of sight and allowing it to undergo the distasteful process of rotting and decaying. If he chooses the former course, that is the end of wheat's benefit, but if he chooses the latter course, it will reappear in a multiplied harvest. Year by year, farmers sacrifice their choicest samples of grain, being content to bury them in the earth instead of exposing them for sale in the market. When one uses wheat for immediate gratification, that terminates its life immediately, but when he plants it to produce a new crop, it achieves its richest development and accomplishes its most fruitful goal. That happened with Jesus; it happens with those who follow Him.

Fruitfulness: of what does it consist?

John 12:26 expresses the essence of fruitfulness. It consists of serving the Lord Jesus, following Him, continuing in His presence, and receiving honor from the Father. In a real sense, fruitfulness is a reward for thinking of oneself as dead in the realm of earthly values and alive in that realm where eternal values prevail.

Jesus said, 'If anyone serves Me, let Him follow Me' (John 12:26a). In inviting people to follow Him earlier, He connected that invitation in Galilee with taking up one's cross (Matt. 10:38). In the region of Caesarea-Philippi He made the same connection (Matt. 16:24 = Mark 8:34 = Luke 9:23), as He did also in His Perean ministry (Luke 14:27). To follow Christ is synonymous with taking or bearing one's cross, a symbolical reference to death and a reminder of how one views himself/herself in relation to temporal concerns and values. But that is only the first half of the picture.

The other half is the rewarding part for such an outlook, the prospect of being with Christ constantly: 'and where I am, there My servant will also be' (John 12:26b). That is the positive side of the self-concept; that is life in the fullest sense of the word. As a part of the Great Commission, Jesus promised to be with His followers always, including the remainder of their days on earth (Matt. 28:20). He also promised them the privilege of His presence after His return to take them to the Father's house (John 14:3). What greater riches in life can anyone expect than to enjoy the presence of the Savior forever.

Yet that is not the complete picture of fruitfulness. When Jesus spoke of His own need to bear fruit, He did so in terms of doing the will of the one who sent Him and finishing His work (John 4:34). That entailed fields that were white for harvest, laboring, sowing, reaping, and gathering fruit to eternal life (John 4:35-38). Bearing fruit in this sense means impacting the lives of people to draw them to Christ for salvation. Jesus accomplished such fruit-bearing through His exemplary life and through His words. He expects His disciples to bear fruit in that same sense.

He elaborated on this goal when speaking of the vine and the branches (John 15:1-5). He taught that the one who abides in Him will bear much fruit just as will a branch that remains attached to the vine. Jesus is the vine, and as long as a branch is attached, the life of the vine will flow into that branch and produce fruit. First of all, fruit enhances the quality of life of the branch, and then through that life produces fruit in the lives of others. Paul wanted to bear fruit among the readers of his epistle to the Romans: 'Often I purposed to come to you . . . that I might have some fruit also among you just as also among the rest of the Gentiles' (Rom. 1:13). In accord with that purpose he declared his readiness to preach the gospel in Rome (Rom. 1:15). He exemplified how a servant can and should bear fruit.

To climax His allusion to fruit-bearing, Jesus promised His servants that they would receive honor from the Father: 'If anyone serves Me, the Father will honor Him' (John 12:26). This promise adds to the dimensions of fruit-bearing in that bearing fruit through serving Christ is not only a responsibility, it is also a reward. What higher honor can one receive than honor from the Creator of the universe? That supercedes all other recognitions and achievements.

Jesus and the death-life paradox in Christian self-concept

The previous four chapters of this work, along with this one, have emphasized how Jesus repeatedly challenged His listeners with the need to think of themselves in a certain way.

(1) They needed to think of themselves as dead in matters pertaining to this earthly, temporal life. He expressed this need in several ways: taking, taking up, or bearing his cross (Matt. 10:38; 16:24; Luke 14:27), denying oneself (Matt. 16:24), losing one's temporal life for Jesus' sake (Matt. 10:39; 16:25; 17:33), hating his own temporal life (Luke 14:26; John 12:25), and learning from the principle of the death of a seed (John 12:24).

(2) They needed to think of themselves as alive in matters pertaining to spiritual, eternal life. He conveyed this to His listeners in several ways also: being worthy of Christ (Matt. 10:37), following or coming after Christ (Matt. 10:38; 16:24; Luke 14:27; John 12:26), finding his spiritual, eternal life (Matt. 10:39; 16:25), being Christ's disciple (Luke 14:26-27), preserving one's life alive (Luke 17:33), bearing much fruit (John 12:24), and protecting one's life to life eternal (John 12:25).

The two seemingly conflicting views of oneself are indeed paradoxical. Yet the paradox resolves itself because the two perspectives deal with two different realms, two realms that exist in every person's life. One is the sphere of matters that relate to time—the temporal—while the other sphere is that of the non-temporal—the eternal. One realm by its nature is limited to a person's limited life-span on earth, but the other spans a life that will not end in physical death. Jesus encouraged His listeners to focus on the latter realm in their moments of decision. He marked this self-concept as the beginning of Christian discipleship.

William Tyndale furnishes a vivid illustration of the principle Jesus taught in John 12:24—i.e., the law of the seed is the law of life. Tyndale's firm conviction of the need for Christians to have God's Word to study caused him to move ahead and become the first to translate the Greek New Testament into English. To do so, however, he had to leave his native England because of opposition from the organized church of that day. After facing continued opposition to his project on the continent of Europe, he finally completed the work in 1526. He had copies shipped back to England where the Bishop of London tried to seize and burn them as fast as he could. Tyndale completed a revision of his New Testament in 1534, and also translated portions of the Old Testament. In 1535 he was kidnapped, tried, and found guilty of heresy because of his translation, and was executed in 1536, first by being hung and then by being burned. Ironically, an English version that drew heavily from his work was in circulation in England with the king's permission a few months before his death, but word did not reach his captors on the continent in time to halt the execution.

Tyndale's translation was excellent, the King James Version of 1611 retaining over ninety percent of it. Twentieth-century revisions of the King James Version have also retained large portions of it. As a result, Tyndale's work has impacted countless thousands, even millions, of lives through the centuries since Tyndale, just one example of a grain of wheat that fell to the ground and died. The magnitude of Tyndale's fruitfulness for God through the spreading of His Word is beyond estimation. Because of the

gospel, Tyndale did not love his life all the way to his death so that the Bible might become available in my language. It reached me and probably most who read these words through his practice of the death-life paradox in Christian self-concept.

The following chart summarizes the discussion above and emphasizes the critical importance of the death-life paradox in Christian self-concept:

THE PROCESS OF BEARING FRUIT		
2 possibilities for wheat	*2 possibilities for wheat*	*2 possibilities for disciples*
1. the decision: to be eaten	**1. the decision:** not to experience the cross, no death	**1. the decision:** loving life in this world, no death
2. results: no more wheat	**2. results:** no further life	**2. results:** no fruit and no further life
1. the decision: to be sown	**1. the decision:** to be crucified, death as the Lamb of God	**1. the decision:** hating life in this world, death for Christ's sake
2. results: more wheat	**2. results:** life for Himself and the world	**2. results:** protecting life to life eternal, being with Christ, impacting people for Christ, honor from the Father

Chapter 9

FULFILLING A BROAD RANGE OF CHRISTIAN RESPONSIBILITIES

Romans 12:1-2

Romans 12:1-2

[1] I urge you therefore, brothers, by the mercies of God, to present your bodies a living, holy sacrifice, acceptable to God, your reasonable service. [2] And stop being conformed to this world, but keep on being transformed by the renewing of your mind, that you may prove what the will of God is, the good and acceptable and perfect one.

Romans has much to say about the death-life paradox in Christian self-concept in addition to Romans 6:1-14, but we must content ourselves with looking at just one more passage. Romans 12:1-2 is familiar to most Christians.

Connections with Romans 6:1-14
At this point in his epistle Paul turns from discussions that are more doctrinal in nature to devote most of the remainder of the letter to items that are more practical. His 'therefore' in verse 1 gathers together not only his defense of God's dealings with Israel in Romans 9–11, but also the far-reaching doctrinal truths developed in the first eight chapters. Connections between Romans 12 and Romans 6 are particularly noticeable.

(1) In Romans 6:12-13 Paul issued prohibitions and a command that strongly resemble his plea in Romans 12:1. Earlier he commanded readers not to let sin reign in their mortal body and not to present their members as instruments of unrighteousness to sin (Rom. 6:12-13a). Then he commanded them to present themselves to God (Rom. 12:13b), using the same word that he uses in Romans 12:1 when beseeching readers to present themselves as a sacrifice to God. He is obviously following up on his earlier directive with a further persuasion to commit their bodies and their whole beings to the one whose grace has provided forgiveness and imputed righteousness.

(2) The manner of presentation in chapter 12 furnishes another connection with Romans 6: 'as a living sacrifice.' Mention of a sacrifice cannot help but recall the reckoning of Romans 6: 'Consider yourselves to be dead to sin.' A sacrifice stands for death, recalling Christ's death as a sacrifice for our sins. A living sacrifice is another way of expressing the death-life paradox as the way to view oneself. One might express the same concept by speaking of a living corpse, living because of resurrection with Christ and a corpse because of being crucified with Christ. This combination is another expression of the paradox in Romans 6:11: 'Consider yourselves to be dead to sin, but alive to God in Christ Jesus.' Paul's exhortation as to the manner of how one presents himself to God involves the same paradox: conceiving of oneself as dead

with Christ and yet alive with Christ. That is the true status of the believer, one that he should contemplate constantly. That is the Christian view of self.

(3) The use of 'reasonable service' in Romans 12:1 presents another link to Romans 6, verse 11 in particular. The Greek word translated 'reasonable' builds on the same root as the verb for 'reckon' or 'consider' in Romans 6:11. Both refer to a mental operation, that is, how a person is to think. The Greek word is the source of our English word 'logical.' It accords with biblical logic for a Christian to present himself to God as a living sacrifice, as one who is both dead and alive. The old man died with Christ and the new man was raised with Him when He rose from the dead. That is the only reasonable way to serve and worship the living God. Coupled with this directive toward mental apprehension comes another reference in Romans 12:2 where Paul commands readers to keep on being transformed through the renewing of their minds. A conscious viewing of oneself in relation to the death-life paradox is an ongoing necessity. We must acclimate our minds to continue thinking in terms of death in relation to certain baser motives and activities and in terms of life in cultivating certain positive desires and undertakings. As Paul wrote to the Philippians in a similar vein: 'Finally, brethren, whatever is true, whatever is honorable, whatever is right, whatever is pure, whatever is lovely, whatever is of good repute, if there is any excellence and if anything worthy of praise, let your mind dwell on these things' (Phil. 4:8).

As our discussion continues, we will see other reasons for concluding that Romans 12:1-2 picks up threads of thought that Paul suggested earlier in Romans 6:1-14.

The 'why', 'how to', and 'what' of Christian sanctification
Romans 12:1-2 are very familiar verses to Christians whose goal is holy living. A closer examination of the verses will reflect three aspects of man's immaterial make-up that speed him in his quest for that goal: his motivations for seeking sanctification (the 'why'), his decisions in reaching that goal (the 'how to'), and his mental framework to assure that he will succeed (the 'what').

The motivational aspect (the 'Why')

Why should Christians put themselves completely at God's disposal? That is a legitimate question. Many other forces in this world are soliciting people to sell themselves out for this or that cause. Why should we respond to God's invitation to give ourselves to Him rather than one of these other entities?

Paul's answer to that question is gratitude to God. Romans 12:1 specifies this motivation in two ways, first in the word 'therefore' and second in the phrase 'through the mercies of God.' 'Therefore' recalls the grace of God that has provided forgiveness of sins and eternal life (Romans 1–8) and God's faithful dealings with Israel and Gentiles (Romans 9–11). Only God's mercies could account for the availability of His salvation to everyone who believes in Christ. In spite of human depravity (Rom. 1:18–3:20), He has provided for our justification (Rom. 3:21-5:21), our sanctification (6:1–8:17), and our glorification (8:18-39). Those are surely among the mercies for which we must thank God and because of which we must give ourselves to Him as living sacrifices.

Further, add to that God's faithfulness to His promises to Israel as rehearsed in Romans 9–11. If He had broken His promises to national Israel, we would have no assurance that He would not break His promises to everyone. But He has not broken those promises. Chapters 9–11 assure readers that natural branches have been broken off only temporarily that those of us who are not branches of the olive tree by nature could be grafted into the tree (Rom. 11:15-24). A God whose promises are that reliable should certainly evoke thanksgiving from those who are depending on His promises. 'God has shut up all to disobedience that He might have mercy on all' (Rom. 11:32).

That combination of benefits provides us with the ultimate motivation to show our gratitude to Him by responding to the apostle's plea in Romans 12:1-2.

The volitional aspect (the 'How to')

Not only does the exhortation of Romans 12:1 stimulate our motivation. It also challenges our wills to make the right decision in turning ourselves over to God: 'I urge you . . . to present your bodies' (Rom. 12:1). Several features tie this recommendation closely to Paul's prohibitions and command in Romans 6:12-13. In the earlier passage he commands rather than exhorts, but the substance is the same, i.e., that of yielding oneself to God. The Greek word translated 'present' in 12:1 is the same as the one used twice in 6:13 and in 6:19 and once in 6:16. Its verb tense speaks of the same once-for-all commitment as the verb tense in the second part of Romans 6:13. That commitment for some may come at the moment of initial salvation, but for most believers it is a decision to be made subsequent to becoming a Christian. Notice five uses of the same word in Romans 6:

Neither continue *presenting* your members as instruments of unrighteousness to sin, but *present* yourselves to God as those alive from the dead and your members as instruments of righteousness to God (Rom. 6:13).

For as you *presented* your members as slaves to uncleanness and to lawlessness, so now *present* your members as slaves to righteousness for holiness (Rom. 6:19).

Do you not know that the one to whom you *present* yourselves as slaves for obedience, you are slaves to the one you obey, whether of sin to death or of obedience to righteousness (Rom. 6:16).

Clearly the apostle in Romans 12 is following up on his treatment of Christian sanctification that he began in Romans 6.

As confirmation of the connection, the word for 'bodies' in 12:1 is the same as used in 6:12: 'Therefore stop letting sin reign in your mortal *bodies* to obey its lusts.' In that earlier passage the noun is interchangeable with 'yourselves' which is used several times in chapter 6 (compare 6:12, 'bodies,' with 6:11 and 6:13, 'yourselves'). That correspondence shows that the writer was not thinking in terms of limiting the exhortation to the physical side of man's existence, but was referring to his whole person.

The fact that Paul uses no more commands or exhortations

connected with Christian behavior between the end of chapter 6 and the beginning of chapter 12 is another reason for deducing that Romans 12:1 begins a development and detailing of what Romans 6:12-13 entails. In the earlier portion of the epistle, he did not specify particular areas of conduct involved in sanctification, but in Romans 12–15 he does that. Romans 12:1-2 introduces the four chapters by taking the readers' attention back to the beginning of his discussion of sanctification and resuming what he began to say there. The two verses seek to trigger volitional responses from readers to commit themselves to God as a key to fulfilling a wider range of responsibilities.

The intellectual aspect (the 'What')
A misunderstanding of the intellectual part of Romans 12:1 has probably contributed more confusion to and interference with a Christian pursuit of sanctification than anything. In a Christian's making that once-for-all decision to give himself/herself to God, he/she needs an intelligent understanding of the basis for that commitment. Otherwise, the commitment will be very short-lived. Romans 12:1 alludes to this understanding when speaking of 'reasonable' service. Some translations translate the word 'spiritual,' but in light of this passage's connections with Romans 6, a word referring to the intellect is a more likely translation. Note the connection with the word 'reckon' or 'consider' in Romans 6:11 that was referred to earlier in this chapter.

Presenting our bodies to God is the only rational or logical service we can render. That meaning aligns well with Romans 12:2, which commands us to be transformed by the renewing of our minds. If we want our commitment to be lasting, we must think right or reasonable thoughts. That is the only way we can present 'a living, holy, acceptable-to-God sacrifice,' as a literal rendering of the latter part of verse 1 reads.

Paul characterizes the sacrifice in three ways. The last of the three, 'acceptable-to-God,' expresses the ultimate goal of one's regenerate nature. Living a life that is pleasing to the one who has brought a person from darkness to light represents the highest attainment possible. 'Holy,' the second characterization of the sacrifice, describes the life that leads to pleasing God. Holiness is another name for sanctification. It is a state of being conformed to the image of Christ toward which we as believers should be progressing constantly. Incidentally, twice in Romans 6 Paul alludes to this state. In 6:19 he commands readers to present their members as slaves to righteousness leading to holiness or sanctification, and in 6:22 he speaks of their liberation from sin and enslavement to God in order to have fruit to holiness or sanctification. This is a further tie-in of Romans 12 with Romans 6.

The third characterization of the sacrifice is that it is living. In Paul's terminology 'sacrifice' has two uses. One is to refer to the generous giving of material substance by Christians as in Philippians 4:18. The other is to refer to Christ's death as a sacrifice as in Ephesians 5:2: 'walk in love as Christ also loved us and gave Himself for us as an offering and a sacrifice to God for a fragrant aroma.' The latter meaning is clearly in view here, the meaning of a sacrificial death. In the context of Romans and especially in light of the multiple connections between Romans 6 and Romans 12, the sacrificial death of Christ must be in view. Stated another way, present your bodies as a 'sacrifice' is simply a restatement of Romans 6:11a, 'reckon yourselves to be dead with respect to sin,' because the death Christ died was your death too.

The other part of the expression, 'living,' picks up a deep theological thread of Romans. It returns to the idea of the 'newness of life' in Romans 6:4, the life that the believer enjoys with the risen Christ (e.g., Rom. 1:17; 6:13; 8:13b). It renews the command of Romans 6:11b to reckon oneself as 'living with respect to God in Christ Jesus,' because His resurrection was the resurrection of believers too.

This, then, is the double picture that Christians are to have of themselves, a death-life paradox. Without it, consistent Christian behavior is impossible. That is why the apostle returns to that picture so often as we are yet to see in 2 Corinthians 4 and 5, Philippians, and Ephesians, and as we have already seen in Romans 6, Colossians, and Galatians. The double picture does not mean that Christians have dual personalities. Each one is still just one person, but that person has two sets of inclinations as part of that one personality. The higher side is the new man, who, reinforced by the power of the Holy Spirit, can prevail over the lower set of inclinations. The lower side is the flesh, sometimes called the old man or residual sin. The conflict between the lower and higher sides is the battle waging within his being that Paul speaks of in Romans 7:14-25. The way to give the new man victory in this battle is to count on the death of the flesh with Christ and on the newness of life of the new man identified with Christ (Eph. 4:22-24).

This way of thinking about oneself is contrary to the popular secular model that dominates our world today. That is the self-love cult that advocates that we believe nothing but good about ourselves. That mode is proving its spiritual bankruptcy by breeding a large segment of self-centered people whose lifestyles reflect little, if any, self-sacrificing love for God and others. The biblical pattern of self-concept is also contrary to the other secular model, sometimes called 'worm anthropology.' This model dwells on that aspect of my being that is so thoroughly sinful, leading to self-pity and depression. Neither secular model has support from Scripture.

The true self-perception gives full recognition that the sinful 'me' stands as crucified with Christ and has no more claims to my allegiance and that the new man is none other than the life of the resurrected Christ being allowed freedom to manifest itself through me. Worm theology is wrong because my old man is dead. 'Self-love' proponents are wrong because my new man is none other than the risen Christ. The paradoxical nature of my being requires that I constantly examine my inclinations to define which side of my being is the origin of each inclination. Is the flesh leading me into this course of action, or is the new man doing so? We can quickly recognize many impulses as coming from the former, such as thoughts of lying, stealing, and the like. The disguised impulses are those that will often trip us up. These may often come in the form of thinking that the end justifies the means. We must be alert for subtle deceptions. A closer analysis of ourselves beforehand could save us from many spiritual tragedies. Recognizing deceptions for what they are, we can allow the risen Christ within to respond to the challenge.

The key to fulfilling a broad range of responsibilities
To do right, we must think right. That is why Paul prefaces the practical portion of Romans (Rom. 12:3–15:13) with words in Romans 12:1-2 about Christian self-concept. The broad range of Christian duties for which this concept is the basis include the following:

1. Conduct in humility in using one's spiritual gifts (Rom. 12:3-8)
2. Conduct in love toward others, believers and unbelievers (Rom. 12:9-21)
3. Proper respect for human governments (Rom. 13:1-7)
4. Proper fulfillment of private obligations (Rom. 13:8-10)
5. Proper personal response to sinful inclinations (Rom. 13:9-14)
6. Proper responses in areas of disputed activity (14:1–15:13)
   a. Recognizing the principle of freedom in Christ (14:1-12)
   b. Recognizing the principle of not offending others (14:13–15:3)
   c. Glorifying God through unity (15:4-13).

The Roman church of Paul's day needed to improve their walk with God in these specific areas.

The improvement would be a part of their growing sanctification and conforming to the image of Christ. In order to practice higher standards of humility, love, submission to government, faithfulness in fulfilling private obligations, personal purity, and respect for others in matters that were doubtful, they needed the right concept of themselves as having died with Christ and having been raised with Him. That self-concept is at the root of lasting Christian commitment and sanctification.

Years ago, while stationed at a U. S. Army post on an island in the southwest Pacific Ocean, I met a civilian worker who had left the United States to come to this island for the specific purpose of giving the gospel to the people of the island. Riding in her automobile one day, I was intrigued by the words pasted on her dashboard: 'Even Christ did not please Himself' (Romans 15:3a). Christ's goal of not offending others in order to please Himself had become her life verse. She had chosen not to please herself so that her life could be a blessing to other people. But something went wrong. She became involved sexually with an Air Force officer who was serving on the island, to the point that she was obsessed with the man. She could think of nothing or no one else. Her objective in coming to that island was lost in the turmoil of trying to satisfy her fleshly inclinations through involvement with this officer.

What caused this radical change in the woman's motivations? She failed to let her mind keep on being renewed with thoughts of her death and resurrection with Christ. She had forgotten that those fleshly impulses that kept driving her relationship with this non-Christian officer had died when Christ died. She failed to think of herself in those terms. She also failed to think of herself in terms of letting Christ live His resurrection life through her, a self-concept that would have driven her to pursue her original purpose of proclaiming Christ to the people of the island. She had originally gone there with the very noble purpose of dedicating herself to do God's will, but her dedication did not have the solid foundation of presenting herself to Christ as a living corpse, of thinking of herself as having died with Christ and having been raised to new life with Him. Maintaining the biblical, Christian view of ourselves is the only safeguard against letting happen to us what happened to this Christian lady on that Pacific island.

See Chart overleaf

The following chart summarizes the discussion above and emphasizes the critical importance of the death-life paradox in Christian self-concept:

Romans 12:1-2 the Sequel to Romans 6—Christian Sanctification:

Presenting Oneself to God as a Living Sacrifice (Rom. 12:1) =

Reckoning Oneself to be Dead to Sin and Alive to God (Rom. 6:11)

3 aspects of the inner life that contribute to sanctification:		
	1. Motivational (the "why")	1. Our gratitude to God for His mercies
	2. Volitional (the "how to")	2. Our gratitude moves our wills to obey God's commands and think reasonably
	3. Intellectual (the "what")	3. The reasonableness of considering ourselves a living [i.e., alive with Christ] sacrifice [i.e., dead with Christ] dominates the renewing of our minds

Chapter 10

Failing
Successfully

2 Corinthians 4:7-15

2 Corinthians 4:7-15

⁷*But we have this treasure in earthen vessels, that the excellence of the power may be of God and not from us; ⁸we are afflicted in every way but not crushed, in doubt but not in despair, ⁹persecuted but not forsaken, cast down but not destroyed, ¹⁰always carrying about in the body the dying of Jesus, that the life of Jesus also may be manifested in our body. ¹¹For we who live are always being given over to death for Jesus' sake, that the life of Jesus also may be manifested in our mortal flesh. ¹²Therefore death works in us, but life in you. ¹³But having the same spirit of faith, according to what is written, 'I BELIEVED, THEREFORE I SPOKE,' we also believe, therefore also we speak, ¹⁴knowing that He who raised the Lord Jesus will raise us also with Jesus and will present us with you. ¹⁵For all things are for your sakes, that the grace when it increases thanksgiving through more people may abound to the glory of God.*

In 1 Timothy 4:16, Paul instructed Timothy to pay attention to himself. Paying attention to oneself is something that we all do automatically. Everyone does it without even trying. The question is, How does one pay attention to himself in the right way? There are many wrong ways, but only one right way.

Timothy had a good example to follow in being attentive to himself the right way. He had Paul to follow in learning proper self-attentiveness. We too can profit from Paul's example. Among the many illustrations of wholesome Christian living that Paul left us is 2 Corinthians 4:7-15 where he explores two extremes in serving others: hopeless failure and overwhelming success. He ranges everywhere from the depths of despair to the heights of victory. Paul experienced a 'victorious loss' in his service. Though on the losing end of many situations, he achieved a winning outcome through correctly paying attention to himself. We need to analyze this seeming oxymoron and learn how he did it. In a section of 2 Corinthians where he expresses his relief for the church's reconciliation with himself, he describes the ministry in terms of a number of paradoxes. An 'exegetical enhancement' of his words furnishes an overview of those paradoxes:

(7) In contrast to the exulting experience of having the light of the knowledge of the glory of God shine in our hearts (verse 6), we have the treasure consisting of such light in clay pots. The purpose of this is to evidence the source of our power. The power we have in ministry, a power beyond all possible comparisons, is from God and not from us.

(8) What do I mean by clay pots? I mean that we are fragile and virtually broken when we are squeezed in every way possible, though we have never run out of room completely to the point of being utterly crushed; or when we are at a loss because we are perplexed in every way, perplexed about how to continue in ministry, though we have never been reduced to complete helplessness in finding some way to go on;

(9) or when our adversaries are right on our heels and about to wipe us out by every conceivable means, though we have never been forsaken and allowed to become permanent casualties of the spiritual warfare; or when our pursuers overtake us and throw us

to the ground with all sorts of maneuvers, though we have always been delivered before the death-blow could be inflicted.

(10) In short, we are *always* experiencing in this bodily existence the death-process of Jesus, having this particular goal in mind, that the resurrection life of Jesus may be exhibited in that same visible framework.

(11) To explain what I mean, we who possess this resurrection life are *perpetually* being handed over to death for Jesus' sake, that the power of Jesus' resurrected life may be displayed in our breakable and perishable flesh.

(12) The upshot of all this is that death is working itself out in us, but resurrection-life power is flowing among you through the supernatural preservation of our ministry to you.

(13) The psalmist exhibited his faith in the face of severe persecution by continuing to proclaim the mercy and righteousness of God. Because the Holy Spirit has imparted to us the same faith as the psalmist had, we continue proclaiming the gospel on the basis of our abiding faith.

(14) That faith produces the certainty that at the return of Jesus God will raise us from death in union with Jesus just as He raised the Lord Jesus, and will present us to Himself united with you.

(15) To summarize, all these experiences are for your sake, with the further aim that grace may multiply through the reaching of many more lives and cause thanksgiving to increase. This will result in attainment of the ultimate objective of everything that happens in the world: glorifying God. The ministry starts with the light of the knowledge of God's glory in 4:6 and ends with the glory of God in 4:15.

Death-life paradoxes

How did Paul do it? How did he muster resources to cope with difficult circumstances? What was the bottom line in his ability to succeed in living for Christ against demoralizing opposition? We can profit from his example by responding as he did when we encounter adverse conditions. We can learn his solution best by observing three kinds of death and the corresponding three kinds of life to which this passage alludes.

1. Three kinds of life

He speaks of life and death in three senses: literally, figuratively, and conceptually. The *three kinds of life* are easier to grasp:

(1) He speaks of the life-concept literally when he refers to future resurrection from the dead. Quite clearly, future resurrection at the second advent is the ultimate bestowal of life. This is the fulfillment toward which all else progresses. Paul alludes to this literal life in verse 14: 'knowing that He who raised the Lord Jesus will raise us also with Jesus.'

(2) He also uses 'life' *figuratively* to designate his miraculous deliverances from various hopeless situations. In a sense, these were resurrections, because he was as good as dead when God miraculously intervened at the last minute to save his life. His figurative use of life occurs in verses 8-9, 11: 'but not crushed . . . but not despairing . . . but not forsaken . . . but not destroyed.' Those situations were miraculous deliverances that he characterizes in verse 11 as 'the life of Jesus being manifest in our mortal flesh.'

(3) Also he refers to 'life' *conceptually,* i.e., to speak of his personal consciousness of union with Christ in His third-day resurrection from the grave. 'The life of Jesus' was manifested on those occasions. The power that raised Jesus was the same 'preeminence of the power' (4:7) that the Lord demonstrated whenever He intervened to rescue him from danger. He uses life conceptually in verse 10: 'that the life of Jesus also may be manifested in our body.'

Paul does not make clear-cut distinctions between these three types of life, but moves from one to the other as though they were merely different ways of viewing the life of believers.

2. Three kinds of death

Corresponding to the three perspectives on life are three perspectives on death: a literal, a figurative, and a conceptual. In that order, here is how Paul portrays them.

(1) Though the word 'death' does not actually appear, *literal* death is implied in Paul's anticipation of future resurrection in verse 14. Some want to deny the verse refers to future resurrection, because Paul elsewhere in his writings, even in the Corinthian

correspondence, did not anticipate dying before Christ's return (1 Cor. 1:8; 15:51-52; 2 Cor. 1:13, 14; cf. 1 Thess. 4:15, 17). Yet these same Corinthian epistles also represent Paul's openness to the possibility of physical death before Christ's return (1 Cor. 15:31-32; 2 Cor. 1:8; 5:8; cf. Phil. 1:20; 2:17; Acts 20:25, 38). This paragraph in 2 Corinthians 4:7-15, where he relives the many life-threatening situations he has faced, conveys the full impression that he anticipated physical death at some unknown point in the future.

(2) Paul uses 'death' *figuratively* in this portion to speak of the personal emergencies that had occasioned special acts of God to keep him alive. Paul was almost always in some kind of danger that threatened either the future of his ministry or his very life. In verses 8-9 of our passage, he graphically describes his narrow scrapes and equates them with death itself in verses 10 and 11. The two in verse 8—'afflicted' and 'crushed'—are probably inner-types of alarm, and the two in verse 9—'persecuted' and 'struck down'—pertain to external dangers. Because those predicaments affecting the outer man are more visible to others, he emphasizes their effect on his body and his flesh in verses 10 and 11. This emphasis on the physical picks up the figure of the 'clay pot' from verse 7 and anticipates the 'outer man' terminology in verse 16 of chapter 4: 'Though our outer man is decaying, indeed our inner man is being renewed day by day.' Yet the outer person cannot be separated from the inner workings of one's being, since man is a unity, not a duality. So what affects the outer man also affects the inner man, and vice versa.

In his epistles, Paul has five other lists of the types of dangers he experienced: Romans 8:35; 1 Corinthians 4:9-13; 2 Corinthians 6:4c-5; 11:23b-29; 12:10. The longest of these is 2 Corinthians 11:23b-29. It too speaks of crises of two types, those originating from within and affecting the outer man and those coming from outside and affecting the inner man.

In the list of 2 Corinthians 11:23b-29 external obstacles dominate. These were of two types: (1) human opposition (i.e., imprisonments, beatings by the Jews and the Romans, stoning, dangers from his countrymen and from the Gentiles, dangers from false brethren) and (2) circumstantial hindrances (i.e., shipwreck, a night and a day in the deep, dangers from rivers and from robbers, dangers on the sea, sleepless nights, hunger and thirst, cold and exposure). The other type of distraction from ministry was internal in nature: the daily pressure of concern for all the churches. The inward anxiety over how his churches were faring was just as much of a burden for Paul as the outward threats, if not more.

The reason why those trials were comparable to death for him was that Jesus called His followers to take up their crosses and, if necessary in their service for Him, to lose their lives for His sake (Matt. 16:24-25). Servanthood for Christ entails launching out on a course that may lead to physical death. Christ's servant must be willing to follow that course wherever it leads, as Paul was.

(3) Just he had for 'life,' the writer also has a *conceptual* sense for 'death.' He uses an unusual word for 'death' in verse 10, *nekrosin*, in place of his usual word, *thanatos* (cf. verse 11). Most understand this word as his way of referring to a 'death-process' that was taking its toll on him from day to day. Several interpretations of the death-process are possible: a gradual weakening of his physical powers while serving Christ, or a daily mortification of his sinful nature, or a figurative reference to the life-threatening perils of ministry, or his consciousness of his once-for-all identification with Christ in His death.

No one of these four needs to be excluded completely, but the fourth must be the conceptual basis underlying the other three. Two reasons support this identification of the death-process:

(a) The implementation of Christ's resurrection life in Paul's mortal experience of trials was purely conceptual as reflected in the discussion of verses 10-11 above. That is what he means by the life of Jesus being manifested in his body. The same must be true of his recognition of these trials in light of His death with Christ.

(b) The thrust of Paul's words in verse 13 points to a conceptual implementation of an actual spiritual relationship. He believed that 'death works in us' (verse 12). He *believed* that, therefore he spoke (verse 13). The Holy Spirit in him generated faith in the power of one who could change death—i.e., the death of Jesus—into life (verse 14). That was his concept of his identification with Christ.

So Paul had the basic conviction that every aspect of his apparent spiritual reversals was merely an outworking of his identification with Christ in His death. That conviction lay at the root of how he responded in his gradual weakening of physical powers, his daily mortification of the sinful nature, and the life-threatening perils he faced.

The death-life paradox in self-concept

The inevitable conclusion about the bottom line of Paul's success in overcoming the obstacles was his ability to concentrate on his co-death with Jesus in the realm of the outer man and his co-resurrection with Christ in the realm of the inner man. Note his statement in 2 Corinthians 4:16: Though his outer man was decaying, his inner man was experiencing renewal day by day. This is what he meant when he spoke of always bearing about in his body the death-process of Jesus that the resurrection life of Jesus might be exhibited in the physical sphere (verse 10), even in this present life. This is another application of Jesus' death and life in the life of a believer. In Romans 6:3-14 the same writer tells of being under grace rather than law as a means of gaining deliverance from mastery of sin. He conceived of himself as being dead to sin, but alive to God because of his union with Christ Jesus (Rom. 6:11). He thereby won victory over sin. In the 2 Corinthians 4 passage before us, he tells of gaining victory over various obstacles in life by the same self-concept: continual concentration on himself as having died with Christ and as having risen with Christ.

Note how Paul did *not* confront his difficulties:

(1) He did not resort to a Stoic rationality that represses an emotional response to the situation. He did not reason that this trouble was simply part of a larger good toward which all things work. He did not pursue a triumph of the rational part of human nature over the irrational by convincing himself of the insignificance of difficulties, no matter how severe. Under this system, a person overcomes hardships by persuading himself/herself that they don't exist. In contrast, Paul acknowledged his

obstacles as very real, adversities that he *felt* very deeply, yet not as severe enough to signal the termination of what God had called him to do.

(2) Nor did he resort to 'toughing' it out, gritting his teeth, and pressing on with the task by using all the human strength he could muster. This 'grin-and-bear-it' attitude, noble as it may be, is not enough. I may possess amazing human attributes of strength and personality, and may tend to resort to them in hard situations, but these will fail sooner or later. They must be replaced by a human-helplessness, identification-with-Christ dependence on God to raise me from the death of this hopeless situation and infuse me with the resurrected life-power of my Savior.

Conclusion

The clay pot must be broken before the life-power of Jesus can be activated in a person who wants to be victorious. This does not mean we must go out and look for trouble to engulf us. Too many have approached life's problems with a chip-on-their-shoulder attitude and have brought troubles on themselves, troubles that are completely unrelated to living for Christ. All we have to do is conscientiously try to serve Him, and the same world-system that made life so miserable for our Savior and for Paul will find plenty of ways to do the same for us. If we haven't experienced such inward heartbreak and/or outward opposition, we can question whether we have really begun to live the Christian life.

This has been one of the hardest lessons I have had to learn through years of Christian living. As time continues to hurry by, it seems that the anguish of having to face determined opposition accelerates. It appears that individuals come along from time to time whose main purpose is to make life miserable for my family and me and to halt the ministry God has called us to fulfill. Likewise, it appears that circumstantial problems to hinder ministry have multiplied. One fall season stands out as one of those particularly bad times: the death of a cherished member of our family, publication of a notoriously biased and vicious misrepresentation of something I wrote, and sudden unfair termination of a longstanding ministry. It seemed impossible to continue after this series of setbacks. Times like this come along, when humanly speaking, we are ready to write 'finis' and give up everything we have started. Though I have never been beaten physically or put in jail, the emotional trauma of such situations is comparable to someone taking a knife and carving a huge chunk out of our insides.

We cry out, 'Why me? Why does it have to be this way? It's unfair! It's not right! He doesn't deserve the good treatment he's getting, and I don't deserve the bad treatment I'm getting! All this heartache is unnecessary in my life for God! There must be a better way!'

If some kind of adversity hasn't come your way yet, be patient, it will, if you are earnest in your pursuit of a fruitful Christian life. How do we respond when adversity occurs? With a vengeful spirit? With a complaint against God? No, but with the same love for the world and submission to God's will that Jesus had. We do not circumvent the trials. Rather we plough through them with life-power that He provides. The pain of adversity is ineffective on the outer man because that man died with Christ. He must stay in the grave while the risen inner man functions in an ongoing unity with the risen Christ.

What is my part? I do not control the timing of the future resurrection of these weakening physical frames. That is in God's hands. I do not choose the method by which He will bring about a rescue from trial, if He chooses to do so at all. This is in His hands too. What I *can* do is to 'keep on reflecting on this concept of myself, that I died with Christ in the realm of the outer man, a death-process working itself out in one way or another as time goes on, and that I live with Christ in the realm of the inner man, a life that is renewing itself on a daily basis in the miraculous rescue He chooses to achieve' (cf. 2 Cor. 4:16; Rom. 6:11). This is not mere self-delusion or the power of imagination to convince myself of something even though it never happened. It *did* happen, and I am simply directing my own attention to the fact that it did. I *did* die with Christ and I *was* raised with Him. The key to tapping this divine resource is right thinking on my part.

The character called 'Interpreter' in John Bunyan's *Pilgrim's*

Progress at one point takes the 'Traveler' into his house of parables to watch the fire that burns ever brighter while someone pours buckets of water on it to try to extinguish it. 'Christian' cannot understand this. Then his host leads him behind a wall where he sees someone else at work, pouring more fuel oil into the fire through a secret pipe. So the paradox is clarified. This tired and suffering humanity has, concealed beneath its surface, the inexhaustible life of Jesus which enables the flame of Christian living to burn ever brighter in spite of the outer man's death.

My sole responsibility in all this is to keep on contemplating my crucified, risen life with Him. This is how Paul paid attention to himself and advised Timothy to do the same. It is also how I must pay attention to myself in facing life's everyday challenges.

The following chart summarizes the discussion above and emphasizes the critical importance of the death-life paradox in Christian self-concept:

Death-Life Paradoxes

	Death	*Life*
literal	[implied by future physical resurrection] (4:14)	'knowing that He who raised the Lord Jesus will raise us also with Jesus' (4:14)
figurative	'we are being handed over to death for Jesus' sake' (4:11); 'our outer man is decaying' (4:16)	'the life of Jesus being manifest in our mortal flesh' (4:11)
conceptual	'we are *always* experiencing in this bodily existence the death-process of Jesus' (4:10)	'that the life of Jesus also may be manifested in our body' (4:10); 'our inner man is being renewed day by day' (4:16)

Chapter 11

SUCCEEDING SUCCESSFULLY

Philippians 3:2-16

Philippians 3:2-16

2Beware of the dogs, beware of the evil workers, beware of the concision; 3for we are the circumcision, who worship in the Spirit of God and boast in Christ Jesus and put no confidence in the flesh, 4although I might have confidence even in the flesh. If any other seems to put confidence in the flesh, I could more: 5circumcised the eighth day, of the nation of Israel, of the tribe of Benjamin, a Hebrew of Hebrews; according to the Law, a Pharisee; 6according to zeal, persecuting the church; according to the righteousness that is in the Law, proving to be blameless. 7But whatever things were gain to me, these things I counted as loss for the sake of Christ. 8Indeed more than that, I also continue counting all things to be loss because of the surpassing value of the knowledge of Christ Jesus my Lord, because of whom I have suffered the loss of all things, and count them but rubbish so that I may gain Christ 9and be found in Him, not having a righteousness of my own which is from the Law, but that which is through faith in Christ, the righteousness which is from God on the basis of faith, 10that I may know Him, and the power of His resurrection and the fellowship of His sufferings, being conformed to His death; 11if perhaps I may attain to the resurrection from the dead. 12Not that I have already obtained, or have already become complete, but I pursue if also I may apprehend that for which also I have been apprehended by Christ Jesus. 13Brothers, I do not regard myself to have apprehended, but one thing I do: forgetting the things behind and stretching forward to the things ahead, 14I pursue toward the mark for the prize of the upward call of God in Christ Jesus. 15Let us therefore, as many as are mature, have this attitude; and if in anything you have a different attitude, God will reveal this also to you; 16however, let us keep walking by the same standard at which we have arrived.

In Philippians 3:2-16 Paul the apostle has laid down some vital principles on which to base a Christian response to success. An exegetical enhancement of the passage will lay the groundwork for developing those principles.

(3:2) A duty that is vital, if your ongoing joy is to remain uninterrupted, is to keep an eye on the people whose distorted viewpoints put them into a class with unclean sacrificial animals. Those are the ones whose profession to be doers of the law is marred through bypassing the doctrine of justification by faith, and whose claim to possess the sign of the covenant is nothing but mutilation of their bodies, because it is void of any spiritual significance. Watch such people, watch them, watch them!

(3:3) The reason I use such strong language is to emphasize that we who have experienced circumcision inwardly are the real spiritual descendants of Abraham. We serve and worship under the direction of the Holy Spirit, boast in Christ Jesus rather than in Moses and related external privileges, and put no trust in outward and earthly merit such as legal observances or physical descent.

(3:4) Yet in viewing myself from the standpoint of those against whom I have just warned you, I can point out far more ancestral and acquired advantages to trust in than any one of them.

(3:5) My inherited privilege is obvious

- from my circumcision on the eighth day like all other native Jews and unlike outsiders who later become Jews,
- from my belonging to the original stock of Israel,
- from my membership in the tribe of Benjamin rather than in one of the renegade tribes who separated themselves under King Rehoboam,
- and from the adherence by my ancestors and me to the strictest customs of the Hebrews, including the Hebrew and Aramaic languages.

My acquired privileges include
- my choice of the orthodox interpretation of the Mosaic law in line with Pharisaic strictness,

- (3:6) my outstanding zeal in leading the effort to stamp out the sect of the Nazarenes who held the law in such low esteem,
- and my maintenance of an observable standard of conduct that was in complete compliance with the law of Moses.

(3:7) Though savoring these benefits during the earlier years of my life, I reverted to the directly opposite perspective that such benefits were a deficit because of being overpowered by my new allegiance to Christ, an allegiance that replaced my loyalty to the law.

(3:8) This 'about face' in the course of my life was not a repeatable momentary change, but it remains my consuming passion to give myself without reserve to continue viewing those advantages of my former state as a liability, because the supreme value of the privilege of knowing Christ Jesus my Lord far exceeds the best of those advantages I formerly enjoyed. Because of Him all my legal advantages and any others I may have accumulated have fallen away in my new state, and I view the whole batch of them as unspeakable filth so that I may gain the advantage of appropriating all that Christ is

(3:9) and prove to be united in a most vital relationship with Him in a way that makes the relationship depend not on a right standing of my own—whose source is compliance with the law—but on a right standing coming through faith in Christ, a right standing whose source is God and which is acquired on the basis of faith.

(3:10) My goal in maintaining this vital union with Christ is to know Him. What I mean by knowing Him is to put into practice the result of that vital union by implementing the power of His resurrection in my outlook and everyday experience and to become a partner with Him in facing the contradiction and opposition of the world which is nothing other than an outworking of my identification with Him in continuing conformity to His death.

(3:11) Through the above-mentioned conformity to the practical implementation of my union with Christ in His death, my goal is to achieve as fully as possible the implementation of the above-mentioned resurrection power in overcoming the obstacles that lie ahead.

(3:12) In contrast with those who may contend they already have this knowledge of Christ in its fullness, I make no such claim even though I have enjoyed a considerable number of successes up to this point. I have not yet arrived at the level of completeness where I need no further development. Instead I continue in the race with the possibility that I may grasp firmly that role for which I have been firmly grasped by Christ Jesus.

(3:13) My fellow Christians, I want to re-emphasize that regardless of whatever claims others may make, I do not conceive of myself in the positive light of already attaining the role Christ intended for me. Instead I focus on doing this one thing and this one thing only: on one side, I do not regard past successes in ministry as having any impact at all on my current spiritual outlook or conduct so as to make me self-satisfied and willing to relax my efforts to win the race, while on the other side, I stretch every muscle in my body in an intense concentration on taking advantage of the opportunities that yet lie ahead.

(3:14) In so positioning myself mentally, I dash toward the finish line up ahead in order to receive the award of knowing Christ that much better, a heavenly award stemming from my union with Christ Jesus toward which God summoned me and continues to summon me.

(3:15) In light of the frame of mind just reflected in my personal testimony, I now exhort those who would classify themselves as spiritual adults—another way of referring to those of the spiritual circumcision of verse 3—to join me in cultivating a general disposition that is dominated by the drive to know Christ in the way prescribed. In the event some of you people prefer some other state of mind, I will await the time when God brings you into agreement with me.

(3:16) While we await the time for further revelation to bring you into complete agreement with my outlook, let each one of you continue walking in compliance with the degree of light he has attained up to this point and thereby maintain our current rate of progress.

Paul invites people to imitate himself in Philippians 3:17. This autobiographical sketch of the great apostle contains many insights into what motivated him and therefore provides us with important lessons in how to think of ourselves.

In one sense, identifying with Paul in this passage is difficult for me. He in many ways was a born winner; I am not. I identify more easily with his self-description in 2 Corinthians 4:7-15 where he reviews all the things that had gone wrong. To relate to one who had so many natural achievements and successes is probably hard for most of us. But we can look around and find things in our own lives that might make us proud from a natural standpoint, i.e., natural successes that we can boast about. With this kind of background, we can learn with Paul how to succeed successfully. We can learn what real success really is and not be satisfied with what the natural man calls success.

One other feature about Paul that strikes a familiar chord is his idealism. He was an idealist. Dissatisfaction with less than the best was built into this man. That made him pursue the complete achievement of his goal, a good example for us all.

As we set our minds to imitating Paul in his quest for completeness and genuine success according to his instructions to the Philippian church in 3:17, four characteristics of his outlook emerge from the passage.

A pragmatic patience (3:15-16)

In leading his readers toward the goal of completeness, Paul surprisingly inserts a pragmatic provision in verses 15-16. His pragmatism was not the same as secular pragmatism that is so plaguing the Christian church and ministry today, but it was a species of pragmatism. His was radically different from the philosophy that says, 'If it works, use it.' His pragmatism was under the control of a strict idealism: 'This is the goal toward which we all aim, and my desire is for you to reach that goal. Nevertheless, I am not going to write you off if you don't agree with me right away. I will continue to work with you patiently until God finally brings you to see the light.'

Displaying that kind of pragmatic patience, he writes, 'Let us therefore, as many as are mature, have this attidude; and if in anything you have a different attitude, God will reveal that also to you; however, let us keep on walking by the same standard to which we have attained' (3:15-16). This is a pragmatism that does not sacrifice principle the way secular pragmatism does. 'Pauline pragmatism' surfaces in several of the apostle's writings, but it never follows the rationale that the end justifies the means. The means are just as ethically legitimate as is the end, because Paul is always careful to divulge his ultimate motivations to those who may not agree with them. He does not manipulate people through deception. Such is a healthy example to imitate.

But what in this case was his ultimate objective for his readers? Toward what achievement was he seeking to guide them?

A passionate preoccupation (3:8, 10, 13, 15)

His goal was to get his readers to *think* in a certain way. Some of the key words he chooses in the passage reflect his attention to developing in his readers a certain frame of mind.

Note the words 'count' and 'knowing' in verse 8: 'I *count* all things to be loss in view of the surpassing value of *knowing* Christ.' The former word at times is translated 'consider, think, suppose.' Through such reflection the apostle compared the relative advantages of his post-conversion state with those he experienced before becoming a Christian. His current evaluation expressed in his counting all things loss follows a series of five consecutive emphatic conjunctions that literally mean 'yes, indeed, therefore, at least, even.' These bring out in the strongest possible way what were Paul's current thoughts on the subject of his relationship to Christ in comparison with successes and achievements of his former life. The latter word in verse 8, '*knowing*' or 'the *knowledge* of Christ,' has a relational dimension to it, but it was a relationship channeled through his intellect, the channel of knowledge.

Another relational 'know' occurs in verse 10, with the same intellectual involvement as in verse 8: 'that I may *know* Him.' In verse 13 the writer dwells further on mental activity in his use of the term 'regard': 'I do not *regard* myself as having laid hold of it yet.' Here he chooses a word that depicts how a Christian is to control his own mind. This is how he regarded himself as an example for others to follow. It is a verb that always tells about what follows from the process of reasoning.

Note the words *forgetting* and *reaching forward* in verse 13. The former verb is middle voice, pointing to an inward act of the apostle: 'causing myself to forget.' He did not rely on memory of past victories. The latter verb applies the figure of intensity derived from a competitive runner to the mental process suggested in the former verb: 'stretching my mind in the direction of what lies ahead.'

Note the words *having this attitude* and *have a different attitude* in verse 15. The verb used twice in this verse refers more to a general disposition than to an isolated thought. It portrays a viewpoint that frames a basis for action. It is not just mental apprehension, but a basic outlook regarding the issues at hand.

All these words fall into a category of terms that describe human thinking, frame of mind, perspective, and the like. Here they pertain to how a person conceives of himself. They tell how Paul thought before he invited readers to imitate him (3:17).

In referring to his own inner life, he proceeded to portray how such an inward disposition is to be sought.

A pursued perfection (3:12-14)
The potential heresy at Philippi included a Judaizing inclination that is very conspicuous in verse 2 plus a perfectionist claim based on a false Christian self-concept that comes to light in verses 12-14. The latter false teaching held that the inner enemy was wiped out at conversion and that a believer is now someone completely different, with no need to combat the debilitating tendencies of his non-Christian past. Paul flatly rejects that error in verse 12, and then repeats his rejection with greater emphasis in verses 13-14. To enforce his insistence that he had not 'arrived,' he compares himself with a runner, so as to convey how strenuously he exerts himself to attain a certain mental self-perspective.

No matter how well he had already achieved that desired mind-set, he always found room for improvement. He found no consolation in victories of the past. Those victories had absolutely

no bearing on what he needed to accomplish in the future. So he followed the pattern of the athlete in straining every muscle in his body, so to speak, in reaching for that perfection of regarding himself in a certain way that he has just described.

But what was that goal toward which Paul pressed?

A positional perception (3:8-11)
The initial mention of this inner quality is in verse 8: 'the surpassing value of knowing Christ Jesus my Lord.' The end of verse 8 has another way of referring to his goal, that of 'gaining Christ.' The positional basis for both is in verse 9: '[that I] may be found in Him.'

The elaboration of what it means to know and gain Christ in this mystical relationship comes in four parts of verses 10b-11: resurrection, suffering, death, resurrection. Disagreement surrounds the meaning of the 'suffering' and the second 'resurrection' parts of the relationship of knowing Christ, but almost everyone agrees regarding the meaning of the first reference to 'resurrection' and the 'death' of the delineation. Those two parts clearly speak of maintaining an uninterrupted consciousness of co-death and co-resurrection with Christ. Paul in these two parts is reflecting on the same circle of thought as he earlier outlined in Romans 6:4-11. Before conversion, the apostle's burning desire was to conform to the law, but becoming a Christian turned that into a burning desire to live out his mystical union with Christ.

Some explain the second part of the description of his mystical relation with Christ—i.e., 'the fellowship of His sufferings'—as the sufferings Paul experienced personally. In that case he spoke of sharing Christ's sufferings in an outward and actual experience. Yet the third of the four parts that immediately follows—i.e., 'being conformed to His death'—shows such to be an inadequate explanation. The affinity between Christ's sufferings on the cross and Paul's sufferings in the service of Christ was so close that Paul regarded his own sufferings as an extension of the death of Christ. In verse 10 Paul so defines these sufferings as 'continuously being conformed to His death.' That is a mental exercise. Like Paul, every believer should regard his identification with Christ as being constantly appropriated and re-enacted in his own spiritual experience of sanctification. The partnership with Christ's sufferings is, first of all, an inner disposition.

These sufferings are, on the other hand, overcome through the same power of Christ's resurrection as it becomes an inner force through a believer's constant recollection. He must reflect on these to receive the inner strength he needs for every kind of challenge.

The meaning of verse 11—i.e., the fourth part of gaining and knowing Christ in that mystical relationship—has been the center of considerable controversy. Some refer it to the future resurrection, saying that it is an expression of humility rather than doubt about whether he would be raised with Christ. Others argue that it reflects his unawareness as to *how* he would attain the future resurrection. Still others say this reflects his usual habit of balancing out divine grace and personal responsibility. All the above suggestions fall short of doing justice to what the verse says. The present context requires some reference to moral and spiritual stimulation such as the results stemming from Paul's mystical union with Christ, about which he has just spoken (cf. verse 9). As has just been stated above, the first three of the four parts of the mystical relationship with Christ in verse 10 belong to the circle of thought found in Romans 6:4-11. Why shouldn't the fourth part in verse 11 do the same? Resurrection with Christ in verse 10 focuses on identification with Christ in His resurrection. Why shouldn't resurrection in verse 11 do the same?

If this is true—and I believe it is—uncertainty still surrounds one other feature of verse 11. Why did the writer use a different word for resurrection in verse 11: *exanastasis* in verse 11 and *anastasis* in verse 10. Possibly he wanted to show a distinction between Christ's actual resurrection in verse 10 and his own practical focus on and implementation of that resurrection here. Whatever the reason, the present context has as its subject present experience which will, of course, ultimately issue in future resurrection.

Knowing Christ at the conscious level of appropriating a union with Him in death and resurrection was the focal point of everything for Paul. His goal was not to feel good about himself. Rather he sought meaning by letting his thoughts dwell on this most vital relationship. His deep emotional state when reflecting on this one responsibility explains the terseness of the expression *hen de* in verse 13, a combination that translated quite literally is 'but one thing.' Paul was one-dimensional, very similar to Jesus' words about Mary's outlook in Luke 10:42: 'But one thing is necessary.' He had a fixation on the need to concentrate on living out his union with Christ.

This brings up the obvious question, 'What is my compulsion as compared with Paul's, or if I have the right compulsion, how well have I stuck to it?'

A personal pilgrimage

Our invitation is to imitate Paul in his quest (3:17). How slow we are to grasp how this most basic of lessons about Christian discipleship and sanctification permeates the whole New Testament! In contrast to Paul's 2 Corinthians 4 application of the basic principle to personal self-appraisal when in the throes of severe adversity, the same writer in Philippians 3 shows how that same principle applies when an individual enjoys outward prosperity and success as humans reckon success. In essence, we learn how to keep an even keel in each situation—not to be overwhelmed with depression in bad times so as to throw in the towel and not to develop a big head in good times so as to rest on our past laurels. In each situation the right response is being preoccupied with and putting into our mental outlook our identification with Christ, our death with Him and our resurrection with Him. That has a 'leveling' effect on our development and service for Christ.

This is not to say that any two of us is exactly alike. God has created us with a variety of personalities and gifted us with a variety of spiritual gifts. We are not to be clones of one another. Each member of the body is necessarily different from all the rest. Yet we all have one area in which we're to be exact replicas of each other: in our attitude or frame of mind that focuses on living out our union with Christ in His death and resurrection, or in other words, in knowing Christ. Nothing can compare with the value of the supremacy of the knowledge of Christ. This is one aspect in which we all are to be on the same wave length.

While studying for the ministry, I had two fellow-students who came from well-to-do backgrounds. One of them took full advantage of his family's financial backing, purchased a home while going through seminary, and was able to support his family working only a few hours on weekends. He was a good student and a gifted speaker and had everything going his way. Yet he failed to let his mind dwell on his union with Christ in His death and resurrection. His contemplations revolved around maintaining the natural advantages he enjoyed in life. After leaving seminary, he went into business, thinking he could combine this with ministry. For some reason, his marriage failed, creating a blemish on his ministry. He did not succeed successfully as did Paul.

The other fellow-student also came from a very well-to-do family. From a natural perspective, he too had everything going his way. Yet we discovered only by accident about his family's wealth. He worked his way through school on meager wages. He humbly depended on the Lord and valued above all else his union with Christ in His death and resurrection. He left seminary and saw many years of fruitful ministry as he continually pursued improvement in the way he knew Christ, that is, in the power of His resurrection and the fellowship of His sufferings, being conformed to His death and implementing His resurrection power in daily living. He was one who succeeded successfully.

The following chart summarizes the discussion above and emphasizes the critical importance of the death-life paradox in Christian self-concept:

Paul's Building-Blocks for Knowing Christ

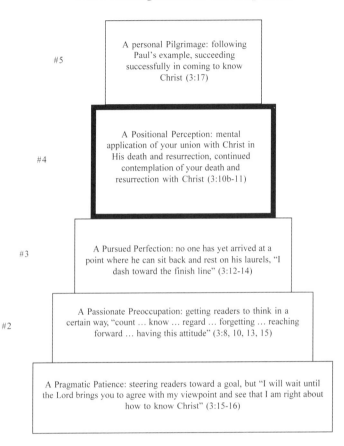

#5 A personal Pilgrimage: following Paul's example, succeeding successfully in coming to know Christ (3:17)

#4 A Positional Perception: mental application of your union with Christ in His death and resurrection, continued contemplation of your death and resurrection with Christ (3:10b-11)

#3 A Pursued Perfection: no one has yet arrived at a point where he can sit back and rest on his laurels, "I dash toward the finish line" (3:12-14)

#2 A Passionate Preoccupation: getting readers to think in a certain way, "count ... know ... regard ... forgetting ... reaching forward ... having this attitude" (3:8, 10, 13, 15)

#1 A Pragmatic Patience: steering readers toward a goal, but "I will wait until the Lord brings you to agree with my viewpoint and see that I am right about how to know Christ" (3:15-16)

Chapter 12

PERSUADING OTHERS
TO
BELIEVE IN CHRIST

2 Corinthians 5:11-21

2 Corinthians 5:11-21

[11]*Therefore knowing the fear of the Lord, we persuade men, but we are made manifest to God; and I hope to be made manifest in your consciences also.* [12]*We are not commending ourselves to you again but giving you an occasion of boasting on our behalf, that you may have something for those who boast in appearance, and not in heart.* [13]*For if we are beside ourselves, it is for God; if we are of sound mind, it is for you.* [14]*For the love of Christ controls us, having judged this, that one died for all, therefore all died;* [15]*and He died for all, that those who live may no longer live for themselves, but for Him who died and was raised on their behalf.*

[16]*Therefore from now on we know no one according to the flesh; though we knew Christ according to the flesh, indeed now we know no longer.* [17]*Therefore if anyone is in Christ, he is a new creation; old things have passed away; behold, new things have come.* [18]*Now all things are from God, who reconciled us to Himself through Christ and gave us the ministry of reconciliation,* [19]*as that God was in Christ reconciling the world to Himself, not reckoning their trespasses to them, and committing to us the word of reconciliation.*

[20]*Therefore, we are ambassadors for Christ, as God entreats through us; we beg you on behalf of Christ, be reconciled to God.* [21]*He made Him who knew no sin to be sin on our behalf, that we might become the righteousness of God in Him.*

When a Christian thinks of himself in terms of the death-life paradox, how does that affect him in carrying out his responsibility for evangelism? Paul the apostle was tireless in his seemingly endless efforts to persuade people to be reconciled to God. In 2 Corinthians 5:11-21 he furnishes insights into what energized his diligence in getting the message of salvation out. His example furnishes lessons for us to apply.

Paul's motives for evangelism

His negative motive
His motives were two in number. The first was a negative motive that he refers to as 'the fear of the Lord' in verse 11. In the verse just before he has reviewed the well-known fact that all Christians will in the future stand before Christ to be judged. Paul had a deep desire to please his Savior (5:9), but the thought of being judged by Christ raised some apprehension in his mind, a fear that some facet of his Christian life might surface that the Judge would find displeasing. That fear prompted him to greater persistence in persuading men to be reconciled to God: 'knowing the fear of the Lord, we persuade men' (5:11). His reverential trust in and respect for the Lord would not allow him to rest in spreading the message of reconciliation.

His positive motive
His other motivation for spreading the good news was a positive one, one to which we would like to give closer attention. He called it 'the love of Christ' (5:14). Christ's love for him controlled him to the point that it would not allow him to live selfishly any longer. Selfish living was Paul's habit before meeting the Savior on the Damascus road (Acts 9:1-19). He persecuted the church to enhance his own standing among the Pharisees. The law of Moses was his guidepost for action, but beneath that, self-glorification motivated all that he did.

He faced opponents in Corinth whose motivations were the same as his before his meeting with Christ. They had questioned Paul's authority as an apostle and accused him of promoting himself through his methods in ministry. They said his gospel was distorted because he no longer advocated submission to the law of Moses. A part of their strategy in attacking him was to boast in their own outward accomplishments, i.e., in externals rather than in invisible spiritual realities. They 'boasted in appearance and not in heart' (2 Cor. 5:12c). They sought to impress men, not God. They were building *their own* personal empires.

'The love of Christ' had changed that perspective for Paul. It would no longer allow him to live for self-exaltation. Everything he did had to be for the sake of others, either for God's glory or for the sake of other people: 'If we are beside ourselves, it is for God; if we are of sound mind, it is for you' (5:13c). Christ's love gained that kind of control when Paul realized that Christ died for all people, and when that happened, all people died: 'one died for all; therefore all died' (5:14c). Christ's death included the death of Paul, as the apostle personalized that historic event to apply to his own life. Further application of the event to himself brought him the further realization that a dead person cannot live for himself because he no longer has life: 'He died for all that those who live may no longer live for themselves' (5:15a). Paul died when Christ died, and found it impossible to live for himself subsequent to that realization. He could not live for himself because he was not alive.

Though he died, his existence did not terminate at that point. Christ died for all people, but He was also raised from the dead by God the Father. That opened the possibility that those who died with Him—and that was everyone—could join with Him in resurrection. In fact, Christ's death had a purpose for all who rise with Him. The ones who rise with Him should no longer live for themselves the way they had before dying, but should live 'for Him who died for their sake and was raised' (5:15b). That is what happened to Paul. Living for the benefit of Christ meant he could no longer live for the benefit of himself. He had to live for Christ and others. This was the way Christ's love controlled him. It all came as he applied Christ's death and resurrection to his own situation by conceiving of himself in a manner consonant with the spiritual realities stemming from those historic events.

Christ's death and resurrection have created an entirely new perspective for human beings. Instead of knowing and valuing people because of their physical and external features, that is, 'according to the flesh' (5:16a), those who are identified with Christ no longer look at others that way. They don't even view Christ that way any longer (5:16b). In a sense it may even be said that the old order of conditions has passed and a new order of things now exists. That's what Paul speaks about in verse 17 of chapter 5: 'Therefore if anyone is in Christ, he is a new creation; old things have passed away; behold, new things have come.' Christ's death and resurrection are the dividing point between the old creation and the new creation. In the old creation a person evaluates on the basis of material standards and external human achievements, but in the new a Christian does so by measuring spiritual criteria, matters of the heart and of divine interest. In speaking of 'the new creation' in 5:17, Paul borrows from terminology that will describe the new heavens and new earth following Christ's return (cf. Isa. 65:17; 66:22; 2 Pet. 3:13; Rev. 21:1) and applies it to the current spiritual state of individual Christians.

In his ministry of reconciliation inner qualities of the heart moved Paul to do what he did. In the new creation God is the source of all things, and He commissioned Paul to the ministry of reconciliation: 'All things are from God . . . who has given to us the ministry of reconciliation' (5:18). That ministry had its foundation in Christ's death, because of which God no longer charged the law-breaking activities of men to their account: 'God was in Christ reconciling the world to Himself, not accounting their trespasses to them' (5:19ab). Christ's death as man's sin-bearer removed that item from the debit ledger against them. Paul's responsibility was to spread the news of the universal reconciliation accomplished by God through Christ: God has 'placed in us the word of reconciliation' (5:19c). God has reconciled the world to Himself, but that reconciliation becomes effective only in the lives of those who know about it and respond by believing in Christ.

As an apostle of Christ, Paul was an envoy of Christ in speaking the authoritative word of God when he pled with his Corinthian readers to be reconciled to God: 'On Christ's behalf we are ambassadors as God beseeches through us, "Be reconciled to God"'

(5:20). The Corinthian church had problems. An element in the church had rejected Paul's authority and, in doing so, had in essence rejected his message of reconciliation. That Paul would call on a group of professing Christians to be reconciled to God is quite surprising were it not for the presence among them of some who had not appropriated God's work of reconciliation in Christ. Such was the case with those who chose to oppose Paul. One cannot claim the benefits of reconciliation as long as one rejects God's official messenger of reconciliation.

Many who have chosen for one reason or another to participate in local church activities today are undoubtedly in the same category as the Corinthian opponents of Paul. Their opposition to Paul is not the same, but they operate in the realm of the old order, not in that of the new creation. They operate in the realm of the outer man, not the inner man (see 2 Cor. 4:16), in the realm of sight, not that of faith (see 2 Cor. 5:7). Their interest lies in looking at the outward appearance, not the heart (5:12; 2 Sam. 16:7). For them the realm of the new creation is still foreign. Like the group of Pauline critics at Corinth, they too need to respond to Paul's plea to be reconciled to God.

Paul capsulizes the message of reconciliation in verse 21 of 2 Corinthians 5: 'Him who did not know sin, God made sin for our sakes, that we might become the righteousness of God in Him.' God made Jesus into a sin offering to bear the punishment that belonged to us sinful creatures, even though Jesus never committed a sin of thought, word, or deed. By doing that, He made it possible for us to become the righteousness of God because of our union with Him in His death. His righteousness becomes ours when we stand before a holy God. By trusting Him, we have the barriers between ourselves and God removed. We become participants in His universal act of reconciliation.

The love of Christ wrought drastic changes in Paul's life that made him a tireless witness in spreading the good news about God's reconciliation.

Lessons from Paul's example

Paul's fear of the Lord

Just like Paul, all believers must give an account to Christ at His future judgment seat. Just like Paul, our deepest desires should be to please Him. If we have been lax in spreading the news about God's reconciliation in Christ, we will experience the great disappointment of being ashamed as we stand before Him to be assessed by Him. That fear should spur us on to greater freedom in opening our mouths to help others receive the benefits of being reconciled to God.

Paul's focus on the unseen

In representing Christ to the world, we tend to focus our attention on outward circumstances. Personalities of various types intimidate us and make us rationalize that this is not the right time or place to tell about Christ's work of reconciliation. We focus on things that are seen rather than unseen (see 2 Cor. 4:18) and fear temporal repercussions arising from our witness. We walk by sight, not by faith (see 2 Cor. 5:7), valuing matters of this earthly existence over those that will prevail after Christ's return. We seek acceptance by other human beings more than keeping a clear conscience before God (see 2 Cor. 5:11). We want to impress people by our outward conduct and appearance rather than by the inward quality of our relationship with God (see 2 Cor. 5:12). In short, we are looking out for our own interests rather than for those of God and other people (see 2 Cor. 5:15).

Paul was not that way. Uppermost for him was the renewal of his inner man, whatever adversity his outer person may have been experiencing (2 Cor.. 4:16). He recognized that items viewed by the physical eye were only temporary and that only those things unseen by the physical eye were eternal (2 Cor. 4:18). He walked by faith, not by sight, as he longed for Christ's return (2 Cor. 5:7). He entertained no thoughts that he tried to hide from God (2 Cor. 5:11). The credentials of his ministry were not of a nature that could be seen only by God, though he did not parade them as his critics did theirs (2 Cor. 5:12). He geared his every action to benefit either God or other men (2 Cor. 5:13, 15).

By maintaining this type of outlook, he inhabited the domain of the new creation where spiritual values prevail (2 Cor. 5:17). That made his fervency as a minister of reconciliation come spontaneously. Spiritual verities were quite real to him so that they overshadowed the visible obstacles that might have interfered with telling others about God's program of reconciliation.

Paul's focus on the death-life paradox
How was Paul able to maintain his focus on the unseen? The answer lies in 2 Corinthians 5:14-15. His motivation stemmed from thinking of himself as crucified and raised with Christ. In verse 14 he introduces his summary of Christ's death and resurrection with two words: 'judging this.' Those two words tell the cause of his being under the control of Christ's love for him. He reached a certain judgment or conclusion about the impact of that death and resurrection on himself. In his background lay an encounter with Christ as he was on his way to Damascus to persecute Christians (Acts 9:1-19). That encounter turned his life around. In the days following, as he reflected on his meeting with Christ, he came to realize that the one whom he hated and whose followers he was so zealous to persecute had made Paul himself the object of His love and had died in his place. The more he thought about it, the more that love became the dominating force in his life. He came to think of himself in a way entirely different from any previous view of himself.

He came to think of himself as hanging on the cross when Jesus hung on the cross. When Jesus died in place of all men, all died. All people were one with Him in His death. Christ's love drew all humankind into a single package and ended an era of human history by taking them along as He agonizingly surrendered His life. Paul was one of those people who were part of that death. When Christ died, he died. That death meant he could no longer place a premium on values of this world. He could no longer respond to human pressure in choosing his actions. He now existed in a separate sphere.

That outlook may sound irrational to some. Perhaps that is why some thought Paul to be 'beside himself' (5:13a). But that outlook was his response to God and His grace in not imputing Paul's transgressions to him. Never mind what other people may think. 'This is the way that God views me, and I agree with Him,' was his thought. A world dominated by evil considers self-centered living as the norm. It views anyone not living for himself as abnormal. Yet Paul proved his normal rationality in his sober-minded and self-controlled behavior toward the Corinthians (5:13b).

If twenty-first century Christians adopt Paul's perspective about themselves, the message of reconciliation will circulate much faster. They will not shrink from human threats, because they will realize that no harm can come to a dead person. The fear of what man may do to me will not overshadow the love of Christ in controlling my life, because my mind is set on my death with Christ. Thinking of myself this way releases me from human intimidation that would keep me from spreading the message that God has reconciled the world to Himself.

My death with Christ is not the whole story, however, just as Paul's death with Christ did not end his existence. Because he was reconciled to God, he was also raised with Christ and that with a purpose. In his raised state of existence, his whole goal was to live for the one who died in his place and was raised in his place (5:15). Joined with Christ in resurrection life meant a life dedicated to the one who was his substitute in death and resurrection. That was Paul's orientation in being part of the new creation (5:17). His dedication to Christ exhibited itself in his concern for other people in giving them the word of reconciliation (5:19).

We should train our minds to think about ourselves the way Paul did even though doing so may make us appear to be odd in the eyes of our contemporaries. We need to dispense with notions of having a good self-image or enhancing our own feelings of self-worth. Self-promotion should disappear from our 'want' list. The concept of our death and resurrection with Christ should replace them.

I died when He died, and consequently self-advancement in the eyes of other people is at best a waste. Why should I spend time seeking to build up a dead person? What good will it do him or anyone else? He is dead and will stay that way. For me to try to convince others how smart or talented he is would be a hoax. Let's put him in the grave and be done with him. Let's not expend our energy trying to improve his standing in the eyes of those who operate only in the realm of sight. John the Baptist said, 'He must increase; I must decrease' (John 3:30). We should modify that a bit and say, 'He must increase; I must become nothing.'

I rose when He rose from the dead. I didn't stay in the grave, but came from the grave with a new purpose. The person who came from the grave is not the same person who went into it because he has a new set of motives. The new motives do not center on the person who was buried. Rather they center on the one who made my death and resurrection possible through His death and resurrection. I am, as it were, living in a new world now, a new world created by His sacrificial act. Everything that belonged to that old world has disappeared. God is the source of all that exists in my new world.

He is the same God who has reconciled us and the whole world to Himself through the death of His Son. Since I in my new role devote myself wholeheartedly to His purposes, I must be busy about spreading the news of reconciliation so that more of my fellow human beings may take advantage of the forgiveness of sins and the new life I have found in Christ. Anything less than that would be to allow that former person to come from the grave and reassert his self-centered life. That cannot happen, however, as long as I conceive of myself as one with the Person who died and was raised from the dead.

As I review Paul's words in 2 Corinthians 5:11-21, one particular courageous individual comes to mind. He came from a broken home in which he received practically no attention from his mother and father. He grew up, developing into the kind of individual one would expect from that sort of background. He developed all the immoral habits through his teens, and eventually became addicted to drugs and all that the drug culture has to offer. When he was in early adulthood, someone gave him the word of reconciliation. He responded positively and entered immediately into a new realm of existence. He no longer sought self-satisfaction. To him what people thought did not matter. All he was wanted to do in his new state was to give to others the same word of reconciliation that had so revolutionalized his life. His passion through every waking moment was to tell lost people that Jesus died for them and was raised from the dead. He planned his whole life around opportunities to evangelize lost people. He was fearless in seizing every chance to talk about the Lord's saving work, because 'the fear of the Lord' moved him to witness and because his entrance into a new spiritual creation put his focus on the reality of the unseen realm where spiritual values prevail. God has honored this man's courage by bringing many into the body of Christ through his testimony. May that kind of courage grip all of us whose trust in Christ has entailed that transition from death to life.

The following chart summarizes the discussion above and emphasizes the critical importance of the death-life paradox in Christian self-concept:

Negative Motive

We persuade men that we may not be ashamed when stadning before Christ at his judgement seat

Positive Motive

Existence in the Old Creation	Existence in the New Creation
path to enter: remain as you are	path to enter: through Christ's death and resurrection
how to inhabit: refuse reconciliation	how to inhabit: be reconciled to God
reason for creation's status: sin and consequent depravity of man	reason for creation's status: Christ's death and resurrection providing for reconciliation
walk by sight (2 Cor. 5:7)	walk by faith (2 Cor. 5:7)
focus on the outer person (2 Cor. 4:16)	focus on the inner person (2 Cor. 4:16)
physical and external values prevail	inner qualities of the heart pervail
desire to live for self	desire to live for Christ and others
fear of human criticism hinders spreading the word of reconciliation	courage expedites spreading the word of reconciliation
motive for behaviou: self-satisfaction and self-promotion	**motive for behaviour: contemplating my death with Christ to the old creation and resurrection with Christ into the new creation**

Chapter 13

REPLACING OLD CONCEPTS AND HABITS

Ephesians 4:17-24

Ephesians 4:17-24

[17]*Therefore I say and solemnly affirm in the Lord, that you no longer walk as also the Gentiles do, in the futility of their* **mind**, [18]*being darkened in their* **understanding** *and alienated from the life of God because of the* **ignorance** *that is in them, because of the hardening of their* **hearts**, [19]*who, having become* **callous**, *have given themselves to sensuality for the working of every kind of impurity in covetousness.* [20]*You, however, did not* **learn** *Christ that way,* [21]*if indeed you* **heard** *Him and were* **taught** *in Him—as the* **truth** *is in Jesus—* [22]*that you put off with regard to your former way of life your old man, who is being corrupted according to the lusts of deceit,* [23]*and that you be renewed in the spirit of your* **minds**, [24]*and that you put on the new man who has been created according to God in righteousness and holiness of* **truth**.

This survey of New Testament portions deals with how a Christian should think of himself. One passage that deserves special attention is Ephesians 4:17-24, because the eight verses contain eleven words that pertain to the mind and its functioning. The translation of the passage on the opposite page has those 'thinking' words emphasized to show the passage's attention to mental processes.

The words 'mind' (vv. 17, 23), 'understanding' (v. 18), and 'ignorance' (v. 18) obviously relate to how a person thinks. So do the verbs 'learn' (v. 20), 'heard' (v. 21) and 'taught' (v. 21). In biblical terminology the nouns 'hearts' (v. 18) and 'truth' (vv. 21, 24) entail activity of the mind too. The nature of the problem in becoming 'callous' (v. 19) is a malfunction of one's mental capacities. This passage of Scripture clearly relates to thinking processes before and after conversion.

The paragraph is relevant to our present study not only because of the frequency of words pertaining to the mind, but also because it gives specific attention to how a Christian is to think of himself.

Ephesians 4:17-24 and its surroundings
The book of Ephesians begins with three chapters of doctrinal teaching about the believer's position in Christ. These three chapters describe the spiritual resources available to Christians, closing with lengthy sections regarding unity of Jews and Gentiles in the church. Chapter 4 begins the practical portion of the epistle emphasizing the obligation of readers to keep the unity of the Spirit. The paragraph in 4:17-24 draws a logical conclusion based on the discussion of unity and mutual dependence among members of the body of Christ in 4:4-16. Since members serve one another in a spirit of love, thereby producing growth in the body (4:11-16), changes in lifestyle reflecting their relationship to Christ are necessary to expedite that growth. Believers need to cease patterning their lives after Gentile thought and behavior as they were accustomed to doing before converting to Christ (4:17-19) and adopt the opposite mentality and life-standards that are characteristically Christian (4:20-24). Love and mutual concern for one another can come in no other way than through vessels who have turned from a decadent life to one that is fruitful.

With the turn-around in intellectual comprehension commanded in 4:17-24, Christians can then clean up particular bad habits that were plaguing the readers of Ephesians (Eph. 4:25 ff.). A proper view of self can remedy problem areas of life such as lying (4:25) and stealing (4:28). Only as a person puts his mind into action along the lines advocated in 4:17-24 can he hope for success in achieving holiness of character that pleases the Lord and has a positive impact on fellow-Christians.

Two contrasting conditions
Christians in Asia to whom Paul wrote these words had a background in raw heathendom. 'Vanity of mind' (v. 17) expresses an emptiness in grasping the real issues of life, an emptiness that had characterized their pre-Christian days and affected the way they lived. A 'darkening of understanding' (v. 18) depicts their blindness that kept them from being able to learn about such realities. 'Alienated from the life of God' (v. 18) refers to the spiritual death that characterized their condition because of blindness. 'Ignorance' (v. 18) and 'hardness of heart' (v. 18) were twin conditions that kept them from obtaining the life of God. Because they were 'callous' or insensitive (v. 19) to spiritual matters, they gave themselves to sensuality in producing every kind of uncleanness in covetousness (v. 19). To say the least, such a use of the mind resulting in that kind of behavior is unbecoming to a member of the body of Christ. More specifically in the present context of Ephesians, that kind of living could do nothing to promote growth and unity in the body. Its effect on the body would be utterly devastating. It would destroy rather than build up. That's why Paul urges and places them under oath—'Therefore I say and solemnly affirm in the Lord' (v. 17a)—so to speak, that they terminate that kind of thinking with its resultant behavior.

He reminds them that they did not learn Christ that way (v. 20). During three years in Ephesus, Paul did not have personal contact with every Christian in the province of Asia, but he assumes that they had heard Christ and been taught in matters related to Him (v. 21). When he spoke of hearing Christ, he clearly meant hearing Christ's representatives. None of these readers had sat under

Christ's ministry in person, but in being taught by Paul and other Christian leaders, they had their minds saturated with 'the truth in Jesus' (v. 21). Verses 22-24 proceed to define three parts of the lessons they had been taught: a putting off (v. 22), a renewing (v. 23), and a putting on (v. 24).

Some have taken verses 22-24 to refer to what happened at the time of the readers' conversion. In trusting Christ for salvation, they had already put off the old man and put on the new man. The ethical commands that begin at verse 25 allegedly find their basis in the positional truths stated in verses 22 and 24. If the putting off and putting on referred to here occurred in connection with initial salvation, they correspond to the uses of similar verbs in Colossians 3:9-10, where Paul wrote, 'Do not lie to one another, since you have put off the old man with his practices, and have put on the new man who is being renewed to a true knowledge according to the image of Him who created him.' The readers in Colosse had already put off the old man and put on the new man. That was to serve as an incentive for them to stop lying to each other. Colossians 3:9-10 refers to a positional change at the time of conversion.

Ephesians 3:22-24 has a setting different from the Colossians passage, however, one that is best taken as expressing an ethical responsibility rather than positional truth. The putting off and putting on in this case carry the force of commands to be obeyed. Paul commands the readers to change their thoughts from the Gentile mold and conform them to Christian norms. In making that change, they will be able to fulfill Christian duties that pertain to external behavior toward others (see Eph. 4:25 ff.). This is the practical side of the positional truth expressed in Colossians 3:9-10.

Verses 22-24 in Ephesians 4 express an obligation to be met by the readers who, though already converted, apparently were continuing to live like the Gentiles around them. Teaching they had received as Christians had already directed them to make that change. Paul's need to reiterate that teaching implies that they had not yet complied: '[you] were taught in Him . . . that you put off with regard to your former way of life your old man . . . and that you be renewed in the spirit of your minds and that you put on the new man. . . .' The Greek verb tenses behind 'put off' and 'put on' indicate a decisive break with the past. The tense behind 'be renewed' depicts an ongoing process. Paraphrasing verses 22-24, we may picture the action thus: 'you ought to put off the old man once for all, continue being renewed in the spirit of your mind, and put on the new man once for all.' The need among the readers was to resolve within themselves to put off the old man right now and to put on the new man right now, and to continue that train of thought about themselves from the point of this initial decision into the indefinite future.

The old and the new
The old man of whom Paul speaks in verse 22 is the same old man of whom he spoke in Romans 6:6. That man was crucified with Christ and is no longer alive. That is positional truth which the believer must keep on reckoning as true in his day-by-day experience (Rom. 6:11). That is the death aspect of the death-life paradox. That is the mental perspective involved in putting off the old man in Ephesians 4:22. To put him off, we must look upon the person who existed prior to conversion as having died with Christ. Ephesians 4:17-19 describes how that old man thought and acted. He was thoroughly Gentile in his whole being and outlook.

Verse 22 describes the old man's ongoing deterioration even after the new man comes into existence: he is being corrupted according to the lusts of deceit. As long as a regenerated person continues in this world, his old man is getting worse and worse. That is why we must take him off as we would shed a layer of clothing. Failure to do so inevitably results in a degraded Christian life that can only go downhill ethically.

The new man is the one who has been raised with Christ when He arose from the dead. He is Christ living in us (see Gal. 2:20), the one who enables us to walk in newness of life (Rom. 6:4). We should consider ourselves alive to God because of our union with Christ in His resurrection (Rom. 6:11). That is the life aspect of the death-life paradox. That is a life of walking in the Spirit (Gal. 5:16), being led by the Spirit (Gal. 5:18), and living in the Spirit (Gal. 5:25). That kind of life is freed from the lusts of the flesh (Gal. 5:16) that so characterized life among the Gentiles.

Replacing the 'old-man' way of thinking with the 'new-man' way of thinking was then to become a regular pattern of living through the renewal of the spirit of a Christian's mind. We can claim the enablement of the Holy Spirit to help us to continue thinking this way. We must remain constantly aware of the potential danger of allowing the old man to rise and regain control of our thinking. We consistently aspire to the potentially high caliber of life attainable while the new man remains experientially in place. Our minds need an incessant renewal along these lines. Otherwise, we will fall back into Gentile patterns of thought.

D. M. Lloyd-Jones has expressed our responsibility this way:

> We are no longer what we were, and the first thing we have to do is to tell ourselves just that! The whole art of Christian living is to know how to talk to yourself. . . . You start your day by telling yourself, Now I am the new man, I am no longer the old man; my old man has been crucified with Christ, my old man is dead, finished with, he is non-existent; I am no longer what I was. . . . You start the new day by saying that to yourself. It will not be said to you, it will not happen automatically.[1]

> When the Apostle tells us to put off the old man and put on the new man, he is not calling for a mechanical conformity, but asking us to put into practice an intelligent change. That is his reason for speaking of being renewed in the spirit of your mind in between the 'putting off' and the ' putting on.' . . . If the spirit of our mind is changed and is renewed, we shall be thinking in such a way that we shall put off the old man, and will put on the new man.[2]

That is the experiential side of the positional truth regarding our old man and our new man. In position we already have dispensed with the old man and put on the new. The tension that we live with is to realize that concerted effort in controlling our thoughts is necessary to activate this position in our everyday practice. Successful Christian living begins in a Christian's possessing a proper perception of himself, the perception of the ever-present danger of lapsing back into the habits of the old man

1. D. M. Lloyd-Jones, *Darkness and Light: An Exposition of Ephesians 4:17–5:17* [Grand Rapids: Baker, 1982], 145.
2. Ibid., 163, 166.

and the ever-present potential of appropriating the higher life for which the new man stands. We must neglect neither the putting off (or death with Christ) of the old man nor the putting on (or resurrection with Christ) of the new man. Both must be objects of conscious apprehension at all times.

Comparison with contemporary teaching about self-image

Contemporary attention to a person's self-image is dominantly man-centered, with only passing notice given to how God enters into an adequate view of oneself. An example of such man-centeredness is David C. Needham's *Birthright—Christian, Do You Know Who You Are?*[3]

Needham's definition of sin is 'the expression of man's struggle with the meaning of his existence while missing life from God. It is all the varieties of ways man deals with and expresses his alienation from his Creator as he encounters the inescapable issue of meaning. . . . The essence of sin, then, cannot be separated from the issue of meaning.[4]' In other words, sin is primarily a human problem in wrestling with meaning, God being a background consideration in that struggle.

Here lies a basic flaw in Needham's system. The essence of sin bears no relationship to man's search for meaning. Ephesians 4:17 speaks of the vanity of the Gentile mind which equates to meaninglessness, aimlessness, or futility. The person without God is not searching for meaning, because he has no purpose such as one who is searching for meaning has. Emptiness and vanity are the core of his thoughts. Sin does not relate to the problem of meaning. It is rather man's quest to be independent of God as indicated in 1 John 3:4b: 'sin is lawlessness.'

Needham claims to have discovered the true meaning of life, thereby eliminating sin, when he denies a distinction between a Christian's position and his experience. A Christian is a saint, not just positionally or judicially, but actually, he says.[5] He even goes to the extreme of relieving Christians of any obligation to obey

3. David C. Needham's *Birthright—Christian, Do You Know Who You Are?* (Portland, Ore.: Multnomah, 1979).
4. Ibid, p. 25.   5. Ibid., pp. 47, 57

Romans 6:11, a command to reckon ourselves to be dead to sin and alive to God (pp. 45, 54, 133). He applies the term 'rationalization' to the act of making Christian-living benefits of Christ's death and resurrection contingent on human faith (p. 237). Yet Paul's writings are full of admonitions to Christians to become in their practice what God's calling has made them in position (e.g., 1 Cor. 5:7).

In taking such a position, Needham rejects the ongoing existence of the old man in the life of regenerated person, believing that the New Testament never exhorts a Christian to put off the old man.[6] From his perspective, only the new man exists in a Christian, that new man constituting his essential, deepest nature. That furnishes Needham the basis for advocating that Christians should have a positive image of themselves.[7]

Along the way Needham denies the imperative force of Ephesians 4:22-24, but he does so without giving close attention to the context in which those words occur.[8] He is wrong in his position on this issue as he is about the new man being the total essence of a Christian's essential, deepest nature. He is also wrong in denying the potential continuing effect of the old man on the life of a Christian. With Needham's concept of oneself, a Christian becomes an easy prey for the old man who is still resident within his being. Unless a Christian reckons with the imminent danger of that old man coming to life to dominate his decisions, a believer becomes a vulnerable target for falling back into the Gentile habits that Paul so specifically forbids.

Ridding oneself of the old by replacing with the new
The practical half of Paul's Epistle to the Ephesians begins with his plea for unity, more specifically for mutual concern and love in building the body of Christ (4:1-16). Recognizing hindrances to that

6. Ibid., p. 56. Anthony A. Hoekema is another who uses the nonexistence of the old man in Christians as a basis for telling them to have a positive self-image ('The Reformed View,' in *Five Views on Sanctification* [Grand Rapids: Zondervan, 1987], 79-83).
7. Needham, pp. 52, 136, 239-263.
8. Ibid pp. 67-68, n. 14.

type of progress, he commanded his readers to desist from ways connected with their Gentile past and to pick up ways they had been taught through their Christian instructors (4:17-24).

Their former Gentile condition was a glaring contrast with the Christian life they had begun, both in thought and in action. To turn their lives around entailed beginning to think differently about themselves. Implied in their Christian approach was the putting off or the reckoning as dead the persons they were before receiving Christ and the putting on or the reckoning as alive the new persons they have become in Christ.

That approach to self-concept differs radically from secular and most allegedly Christian approaches to self-image. The latter are ultimately man-centered, leaving God as a background fixture. The Christian approach takes God at His Word and advocates an ongoing consciousness of the need to keep putting off the old man and putting on the new man.

The human mind is a marvelous creation. It is capable of marvelous achievements. Through applying its capabilities to earning money, some have amassed huge fortunes. Bill Gates in his building of the Microsoft empire is an example of this use of the mind. Applying the mind's capabilities in another way, Cameron Townsend started a Bible-translation movement that has grown into a huge work known as Wycliffe Bible Translators. More basic and more important than either of these uses of the mind, however, is the application of the mind to maintaining the biblical view of oneself. When a person can gear his mind to remembering the death of his old man and the resurrection of his new man with Christ, he has achieved God's primary goal and will have his maximum output in helping build the body of Christ.

One of the great leaders in the church of east Africa illustrates the realization of this potential of the human mind. His background lay in African tribal warfare of the worst kind. He had scars all over his body from injuries suffered in battles with other tribes. He was the embodiment of raw heathendom. He received the gospel and became a believer in Christ. He begin training his mind in the Scriptures by submitting himself to Christian teachers. He went to the

United States for additional training at the institution where I was teaching, earned a terminal degree from another institution, and returned to his homeland to involve himself in reaching his own countrymen with the gospel. He rose rapidly into the leadership of his denomination and has become a powerful force in building the body of Christ in that part of the world. He left his Gentile ways of thinking behind and put on the new man who was raised from the dead with Christ. God can accomplish much through His children who gear their minds to think right thoughts about themselves.

The following chart summarizes the discussion above and emphasizes the critical importance of the death-life paradox in Christian self-concept:

Two Constrating States of Mind

The Gentile Way of Thinking	The Christian Way of Thinking
vanity of mind	dispense with learning contrary to Christ
darkening of understanding	hearing Christ
alienated from the life of God	being taught in Christ
ignorance	the truth in Jesus
hardness of heart	putting off the old man
callous	putting on the new man
sensuality leading to impurity	being renewed in the spirit of your minds
the old man – alive and well the new man – nonexistent life for the old man way of thinking death to the new man way of thinking	the old man – crucified with Christ the new man – raised with Christ death to the old man way of thinking life for the new man way of thinking

Chapter 14

ACHIEVING CHRISTIAN SUBMISSION

1 Peter 2:24

1 Peter 2:24

who Himself bore our sins in His body on the tree, that we, having died to sin, might live to righteousness; through whose stripe you were healed.

Peter devoted a large section of his first epistle to the important Christian quality of submission (1 Pet. 2:11–3:7). He commanded submission to secular government as a citizen in the state (2:13-17), submission in the household as a servant (2:18-21a), and submission in marriage as a wife or husband (3:1-7). To illustrate and enforce the section on submission in the household, he digressed in order to cite the example of Christ's submission (2:21b-24): 'Because Christ also suffered for you, leaving you an example that you should follow in His footsteps; who being insulted, did not insult in return; suffering, He did not threaten, but delivered Himself to the one who judges righteously; who Himself carried our sins in His body on the tree, that we, having died to sins, might live for righteousness; through whose stripe you were healed.'

Submission is an important virtue of the Christian life. Paul matches Peter's attention to the subject by devoting a significant section of his Ephesian epistle to cultivating submission (Eph. 5:19–6:9). He also shows it to be an aspect of love in a portion of the well-known 'love' chapter (1 Cor. 13:4-5, 7).

In introducing his discussion of submission, Peter relates it to the exemplary lifestyle that will shut the mouths of non-Christians and cause them to glorify God in the day of visitation (1 Pet. 2:11-12). In Peter's mind, insubordination—the opposite of submission—was one of the fleshly lusts from which he urged his readers to abstain (cf. 1 Pet. 2:11). God has established an order of authority in every realm of life, including the state, the workplace, and the family. Christians have the responsibility to respect duly constituted authority as part of their proper behavior before God.

Peter's Christological interlude in his discussion of submission shows that Christ through His death provided for us an example of submission, a motive for submission, and a means of achieving that submission.

An example of submission
Peter uses Christ's example immediately after writing about the need for household servants to submit respectfully to their masters (2:18-21a). Masters of households—i.e., employers—are of two kinds. Some are good and kind; others are harsh and unreasonable.

Showing respectful submission to the former type is not difficult, but to show that kind of respect to the latter group runs counter to human nature. Peter is commending those servants who put up with wrongful treatment because of their consciousness that such is God's will (2:19). Servants who experience suffering because of their own poor service and sinful lack of submission deserve no special credit, but those who do good and suffer at the hands of an unjust master or an unreasonable employer, while maintaining a submissive attitude toward that master, find favor with God (2:20). God has called Christians to travel this latter road (2:21a).

We find this hard to accept. Our closest analogy to what Peter describes is the employment we have to support our families and ourselves. We work hard and expect to be treated fairly by our superiors, but that does not always happen. Sometimes we find inequities, with our bosses showing favoritism to less diligent employees who deserve punishment rather than special good treatment. We see others getting raises in salary or extra time off though we work much harder than they do. At other times we get the blame for something that goes wrong on the job while one of the employer's favorites who caused the problem gets a clean slate. Under circumstances like this, can we continue rendering respectful submission to our superiors? We not only can do it; we must do it. That is God's calling for our lives.

Someone will say, 'That's too difficult. I can't handle it.' Peter answers, 'Christ did.' He reviews how Christ suffered for us, leaving us an example to follow in His footsteps (2:21b). Christ did nothing wrong. He was an ideal citizen. He said nothing deceitful, never maligning His superiors (2:22). They insulted Him, but He did not retaliate. He did not threaten those who inflicted great mental and physical pain upon Him. Rather He entrusted Himself to the God who judges with equity and justice (2:23). He went to the cross because of our sins, not for His own (2:24a). He submitted respectfully to duly constituted authority even though that authority was completely out of hand and in the wrong. He did not rebel. He did not disobey. He did not protest that they were violating His rights. He submitted because His antagonists were in positions of leadership through God's sovereign choice. He had to submit to them. That was the perfect example of respectful submission we need to follow.

Household servants, citizens, wives, employees, students, or anyone subject to duly constituted authority, learn from the example of Christ what Christian submission is.

A motive for submission

Obedience to God is a sufficient reason why we should submit to divinely constituted authority, but Scripture does not stop there in supplying motivation. As a climax to Peter's description of Christ's submission, 1 Peter 2:24a reminds us of the price Christ paid to release us from the penalty for our sins: 'Who Himself bore our sins in His body on the tree.' When Christ hung on the cross, He hung there for our sake, taking the punishment that we should have borne. That sacrificial act should evoke in us the maximum degree of gratitude of which we are capable. We should adhere to the divine standard of submission as a response prompted by our appreciation to Him.

The picture of verse 24a derives from Isaiah 53:12: 'He Himself bore the sin of many.' This Old Testament passage predicted the future sacrifice of the coming Suffering Servant of the LORD, a prophecy fulfilled by Jesus in His crucifixion. The primary thought of the Isaiah text is the same as the primary thought of Peter's words: Christ's becoming a substitute for us in taking punishment in our place. The sacrificial system of the Old Testament law previewed His act when the high priest killed an animal on the altar so that each year the sins of the people could be atoned for in God's sight. That animal was a substitute in bearing the penalty that the people deserved.

Jesus brought to a climax those annual offerings of animals when He became the sin-offering for the human race of all time, when He carried our sins in His body on the cross. His offering need not be repeated, however. The death that He died, He died once for all time as it was once for all people. 'Christ suffered for sins once for all' (1 Pet. 3:18). No more annual sacrifices are necessary.

He carried our sins 'in His body.' They were not separate from

Himself. No other agent was involved. This was His personal act, necessitating very persuasively our need to express gratitude to Him by showing submission in various relationships specified in the context surrounding this verse.

If we stop to ponder even briefly what we would have faced if He had not assumed the role of our substitute, we cannot help but respond from motives of appreciation. We read in the last book of the Bible about the awfulness of eternal punishment. We read about the lake of fire that will be the final permanent destiny of those whose sins have not been forgiven (Rev. 20:14-15). We learn of those who will drink of the wine of the wrath of God and of their ongoing torment in fire and brimstone and of the smoke of their torment that ascends eternally (Rev. 14:9-11). Jesus spoke of the plight of the lost whose worm never dies and whose fire is not quenched (Mark 9:48).

By taking our place and bearing the penalty for our sins, Jesus experienced the misery of separation from God that we deserved. We must remain eternally grateful to Him for that. Obeying His will that we submit to whatever authority He places in our lives is a very small thing to ask in response to the debt we owe Him. Jesus not only provided us an example of submission. He also gave us the strongest possible motive for doing so.

A means of achieving submission
First Peter 2:24b discloses the means available to Christians to achieve the commanded submission: 'that we, having died to sins, might live for righteousness.' To a large degree, an understanding of these words hinges on the meaning of the Greek word translated 'died' in this verse. This is not the usual word for 'die' in the New Testament. It carries the etymological sense of 'remove (or depart) from,' and if the context permits, the idea of 'depart from life' or 'die.' The question here is whether the connotation is that of being removed from sins or of being removed from life with reference to sins.

If one chooses the former meaning, the case of the Greek noun translated 'sins' requires a rendering of something like 'depart with reference to sins.' That case of the Greek noun does not lend itself to the meaning of 'depart from sins.' Most probably the sense of the word is 'died' and of the total expression 'died with reference to sins.' This is very close to the ideas expressed by Paul in Romans 6:10, 11: Christ died with reference to sin. . . . We consider ourselves dead with reference to sin. This correspondence presents a strong case for concluding that Peter is thinking of our identification with Christ in His death when he speaks of our having died to sin in 2:24b. When we note in the remainder of the verse the use of the verb 'live,' that seals the case for assigning this meaning to the words.

What are the sins to which Peter refers? Certainly they are the sins that Christ bore on the cross, the ones spoken of earlier in the same verse. But we can probably be more specific in a larger context that elaborates on submission. Peter introduces the whole discussion of submission with an exhortation to abstain from fleshly lusts (2:11) and urges his readers to replace these with good works, the impact of which will bring people around them to glorify God (2:12). The fleshly lusts are attitudes of insubordination or rebellion that are to be replaced by submission in various relationships. An attitude of submission toward governmental authority (2:13-17), household masters (2:18-21a), and marital spouses (3:1-7) is the fountain from which will spring good works to win the onlookers. An attitude of insubordination is the source of not being submissive in the same spheres. Contextually, that most probably is the specific focus of the 'sins' in 2:24 when Peter speaks of our having died to sins. Undoubtedly our death with Christ covers more ground than that, but that is the point of concentration in this section.

Peter was apparently writing to an audience whose Christian lives were lacking appropriate submission. The lack was bringing shame on the Christian communities addressed and reducing the effectiveness of their witness for Christ. Peter reminds them that insubordination was a trait they left behind when they died with Christ. They now have a new life to live with Him in which insubordination has no place.

Peter's point is this: the death that they died and the life that they now live go together, side by side. He does not say such in so many words, but the underlying thought is that their present life is the resurrection life of Christ possessed by having been raised with Christ in His resurrection. Submission characterizes that resurrection life just as it characterized the incarnate life of Christ. The death-life paradox that Peter gives means freedom from insubordination and freedom to submit to rightly constituted authority.

The purpose of Christ's bearing our sins on the tree was 'that we, having died to sins, might live for righteousness' (2:24). The righteousness was the same as He exhibited during His life on earth, a righteousness expressed in His submissive demeanor under the most adverse circumstances (2:22-23). Lest we forget our debt to Him, Peter adds at the end of verse 24, 'through whose stripe you were healed.' The word translated 'stripe' refers to the mark or welt left on the flesh by a scourge. A scourge was a whip of some kind, something akin in our day to a horsewhip. In this instance the singular number of the noun refers to the ultimate mark made on our Lord by the stroke of death. His death fulfilled the prophecy of Isaiah 53:5: 'by His scourging we are healed.'

The surrounding discussion necessitates that this be a reference to spiritual, not physical, healing. We have been healed from the waywardness of sins that plagued us before we became identified with Christ in His death and resurrection. With the healing He has accomplished for us, we are now free to exhibit the same lifestyle that He exemplified, specifically in our responsibilities to civil, domestic, and marital authorities.

To elaborate on the death-life transformation we have undergone, Peter explains, 'For you were as sheep going astray, but now you have turned to the shepherd and overseer of your souls' (2:25). We have died to sins that contaminated us in our pre-Christian days, and have turned to the tender loving care of our great Shepherd who laid down His life for the sheep (see John 10:11; Heb. 13:20) and to the Guardian who serves us by watching over us. Through His sacrifice and continual care, we have the means to be released from our former ungodly habits and to live in a way that will cause those around us to glorify our God as they witness our submissive behavior (see 1 Pet. 2:12).

The whole picture

In the brief span of a few verses Peter has provided us with an example of submission, a motive for submission, and a means for achieving submission. As we face a harsh world all around us, may we give attention to how Christ achieved submission even though mistreated terribly. May we strive to obey God, moved out of gratitude for the supreme price Christ paid so that we would not have to be separated from God forever, and may we constantly keep in mind that achieving His standard of righteousness is possible as long as we remember *our* death and resurrection which came when He died and rose. May we mentally dwell on that truth as we consider our responsibility to submit to government, to employers, to school teachers, to husbands, or any other duly constituted authority. The same lesson applies indirectly to those who are leaders, whose responsibility is to submit to whatever is in the best interests of those whom they lead.

During the first year of my Christian life, I was called to active duty in the U. S. Army. At Aberdeen Proving Ground, Maryland, the second company commander under whom I served was an extremely vulgar man. His language, his moral standards, and his expectations from others were conditioned by his vulgar outlook. He was radically different from my first company commander, who though not a Christian, was a respectable, clean-cut individual. Needless to say, life was different for me when the second commander took over. He could not stand me, even the sight of me, because of the moral standards for which I stood. He did everything in his power to humiliate me. He gave me the worst treatment that he could without getting into trouble with his superiors. He rated my performance of duties with the lowest score he could give me without recommending a court martial for me.

That kind of treatment was hard to take. As a young Christian, I knew little about the Bible, specifically what it taught about submission. If I had only known more about my death with Christ and the privilege of letting Him live His resurrection life through me, I'm sure I could have handled that adverse situation more positively. That part of me that wanted to respond in kind to the bad treatment was the part that died with Christ. The part that was raised with Christ would have handled it the way Christ handled His ill treatment, that is, with submission. In such a way I could have borne a more effective testimony of what Christ had done for me as I lived among non-Christians. That would have been the righteous thing for me to do.

The following chart summarizes the discussion above and emphasizes the critical importance of the death-life paradox in Christian self-concept:

THE IMPORTANCE OF SUBMISSION

The Example	The Motive	The Means of Achieving	The Goal
1. Christ's Submission to Duly Appointed But Unfair Authorities	2. Gratitude to Christ for Bearing Our Sins Leads to Following God's Will in Submitting Even to Harsh Superiors	3. Death with Christ to the Sin of Insubordination and Life with Christ to the Righteousness of Submission	Submission, a Behavioral Testimony to a Lost World

Chapter 15

FOLLOWING THE WILL OF GOD

1 Peter 4:1-6

1 Peter 4:1-6

Therefore, since Christ has suffered in the flesh, arm yourselves also with the same thinking, because the one who has suffered in the flesh has ceased from sin, ²that he may live the remaining time in the flesh no longer for the lusts of men, but for the will of God. ³For the time that has passed is sufficient for you to have carried out the will of the Gentiles, having traveled in sensuality, lusts, drunken sprees, carousals, drinking parties, and abominable idolatries, ⁴in which matter, they think it strange when you do not run with them into the same excess of dissipation, slandering you; ⁵they will give an account to Him who is ready to judge the living and the dead. ⁶For the gospel for this purpose was also preached to those who are dead, that though they have been judged in the flesh according to men, they might live in spirit according to God.

In 1 Peter 4:1-6, Peter follows a second Christological passage with a second allusion to the death-life paradox. First Peter 3:18-22 is a second elaboration on Christ's death in the epistle, the first being found in 1 Peter 2:24-25. This time Peter alludes to Christ's suffering for doing good (3:18-20) and His eventual victory over death through His resurrection and ascension (3:21-22). In 4:1-6 the author builds on that example of Christ to bolster his readers' confidence. They too will win an eventual victory by arming themselves with the same mental outlook as Christ had. That attitude of mind and guiding conviction meant they must follow the will of God by doing good, no matter what the obstacles. Even death itself should not be a deterrent.

Importance of right thinking (1 Pet. 4:1a)

Peter put great emphasis on using the mind. Earlier in 1 Peter he challenged readers to gird up the loins of their *minds* (1:13). In 2 Peter 3:1 he purposed to stir up his readers' *minds* by way of reminder. How Christians use their minds determines their courses of action. Here in 1 Peter 4:1 he directs readers to have the same *mind* or purpose as he has described for Christ at the end of chapter 3. Such a mental posture is the best weapon when doing battle in a world that is unfriendly to Christians and Christian principles. Identifying that frame of mind is therefore of greatest importance.

Christ's mental purpose was to suffer in the flesh that He might bring us to God (3:18). The just one died for unjust ones. He suffered because He did good (see 3:17). He was willing to go all the way to the cross to accomplish a purpose of unequaled nobility. His belief was that the goal was worth the price He had to pay, that of giving His life. No sacrifice was too great in comparison with the good purpose He sought to accomplish. That mind-set is the weapon with which we should arm ourselves to wage warfare in this world, according to 1 Peter 4:1a.

The 'death' side of the death-life paradox (1 Pet. 4:1b)

The reason we should adopt that attitude comes in 1 Peter 4:1b: 'the one who suffers in the flesh has ceased from sin.' Identification of 'the one who suffers in the flesh' has posed a great challenge to

Bible interpreters. Is this person Christ Himself? Hardly. Christ never committed sin from which He could cease. Is this simply a proverbial saying that speaks of the purging effects of suffering? No, because suffering in itself does not have a cleansing effect on everyone. With some, suffering brings greater tendencies to sin. Most probably, 'the one who has ceased from sin' refers primarily to the believer in the sense that through his death and resurrection with Christ he has been emancipated from sin's mastery in his life. As Paul explained in Romans 6:3-11, the death that Christ died was also that of the believer because of the identification of believers with Christ in His death. Christ too was emancipated from the forces of evil by bearing our sins in His body when He died.

In this epistle Peter has already alluded to our union with Christ in his death. In 2:24, when discussing Christ's example of submission, he wrote of our having died to sin. Our union with Christ is such that His suffering in the flesh was also our suffering in the flesh. The cessation from sin of which Peter speaks in 4:1b is another way of referring to the termination of the reign of sin about which Paul speaks in Romans 6:12-13a: 'Therefore stop letting sin reign in your mortal body that you should obey its lusts, neither go on yielding your members as weapons of unrighteousness to sin.' Such a view of self is the same weaponry that Paul designates in Romans 6:13a. That is the only road to the cessation of sin in our lives, both in Romans 6 and in 1 Peter 4. That is the goal of the Christian who thinks about himself in the right way. By ceasing from sin believers assure themselves that whatever suffering comes their way comes because of doing good. They thereby join Christ in suffering because of following the will of God rather than because of committing evil deeds (see 1 Pet. 3:17).

The 'life' side of the death-life paradox (1 Pet. 4:2-4)
In 1 Peter 4:2, Peter continues with another purpose for a Christian arming himself with the right mental paraphernalia and ceasing from sin: 'so that he lives the rest of his time no longer for the lusts of men, but for the will of God.' Here is the 'life' side of the death-life paradox. Peter chose a different word for 'life' here. Rather than the usual word *zaō*, he uses the term *bioō*. Like *zaō*, *bioō* means 'I live,' but it focuses more on the means by which physical life is

sustained. Often in the New Testament, *zaō* is elevated into the ethical and spiritual sphere, but *bioō* refers to down-to-earth, daily living. Peter admonishes his readers not to conduct their daily lives in accord with the haphazard and wicked desires of the secular world. He wants them to be guided by a single principle, the will of God, just as Christ was (cf. 1 Pet. 3:17-18). When they follow that guideline, the life of the resurrected Christ will flow through them.

Like most of us, Peter's readers had in pre-Christian days spent a sufficient amount of time bowing to the persuasion of non-Christians who trafficked in debauchery, lusts, drunkenness, orgies, drinking parties, and abominable idolatries (1 Pet. 4:3). But those days are past for one who has ceased from sin. They have no place in the life that has for its objective fulfilling the will of God. They have no place in the experience of one through whom the resurrected Christ is living His life. A radical change has transpired in the person who has died and been raised with Christ.

Yet that radical change has negative repercussions for former associates in dissolute living. Those former associates find new behavior of Christians strange when believers dump the old 'excesses of dissipation.' Consequently, critics will heap abuse on believers and thereby, by implication, blaspheme the God whose will now determines the behavior of Christians (4:4). Those of us who have undergone a significant change in lifestyle since becoming Christians easily sense the negative treatment about which Peter speaks. Our former friends and even non-Christian family members tried to keep us at 'arm's length' because of our newly discovered devotion to the Lord. In some instances—as appears to have happened to some of 1 Peter's readers—the estrangement escalates into harsh physical measures that may become life-threatening. Similarly in modern times, many a believer in Christ has lost his life because his faith set his life on a new course. Persecution has been a well-known commodity among Christians throughout the centuries just as it was in Peter's day. It comes as a consequence of a change in behavior that brings a person in Christ to reject his old ways and assume a new direction in living in compliance with the will of God. Life in Christ can proceed in no other way.

The ultimate victory (4:5-6)

Persecution in this life is not the end of the story, however. Someone stands ready to judge all people, both living and dead. Those who have made earthly life miserable for Christians will give an account for maligning Jesus' followers and indirectly Jesus Himself. Jesus is ready to judge the offenders (4:5). A knowledge that the Lord will some day pay back those who currently treat them unjustly is an encouragement and comfort to victims of persecution. He is ready to judge right now. That means that the avenging of their suffering is imminent, i.e., it may come at any moment. In 1 Peter 4:7 the writer re-emphasizes the imminence of this coming judgment by pointing forward to the second coming of Christ and the 'any moment' possibility of its occurrence.

One cannot help recalling other instances in the New Testament when persecuted believers have, in light of the imminent return of Christ, received encouragement to persevere in their faith. Jesus told the persecuted minority in Thyatira to hold fast until He comes (Rev. 2:25). The suffering Christians in Philadelphia received much the same advice from Him when He told them to hold fast what they had until He comes so that no one would take away their crown (Rev. 3:11). Paul consoled the afflicted church in Thessalonica by reminding them of the coming righteous judgment of God that will set right affairs on earth, thereby relieving them of their suffering (2 Thess. 1:4-5). In these and other instances, the speakers/writers view the coming of Christ as an any-moment possibility, furnishing readers an incentive to hold on just a little bit longer.

Even the souls of martyred saints in heaven look forward with great anticipation to the day when God will judge and avenge their blood. That is the picture of the fifth-seal judgment when they cry, 'How long, holy and true Master, will you not judge and avenge our blood from those who dwell upon the earth?' (Rev. 6:10). That future cry will come during the seven-year fulfillment of Daniel's seventieth week (Dan. 9:24-27). In that case God informs them of further delay before the avenging of their murderers (Rev. 6:11). But in the case of Peter's living readers, the avenging could transpire at any moment. Hence, the encouragement for them to persevere a bit longer.

Peter offers his persecuted readers every possible incentive to persevere in living for the will of God. He therefore, in light of future judgment, proceeds to furnish them with further rationale regarding their present suffering: 'For because of this the gospel was also preached to the dead, that they, on the one hand might be judged according to men in the flesh, but on the other might live according to God in the spirit' (1 Pet. 4:6). These words raise several questions without easy answers. One question is, 'Who are the dead in 4:6a?' The strongest evidence identifies the dead as those believers who have given up their lives in following the will of God. In other words, they are Christian martyrs. A little later Peter speaks of the fiery trial that will possibly overtake his readers (1 Pet. 4:12) and of their sharing in the sufferings of Christ (1 Pet. 4:13). The 'death' side of the death-life paradox entails a willingness to give up one's life in living for Christ if called on to do so. When referring to 'the dead' in v. 6, Peter speaks of such believers of the past who are now dead, probably having given up their lives for Jesus' sake.

Before death, those dead ones had the gospel preached to them for a purpose: that they might live in the spirit in their relationship with God after having been judged in the flesh while in their relationship with men (4:6b). 'What was their judgment by men?' is another question. Their judgment by men was their harsh treatment by former associates after they terminated lifestyles fashioned after 'the lusts of men' (see 4:1). Living for the will of God caused men to judge them as enemies and to heap scorn and cruel treatment upon them, treatment cruel enough in some cases to produce death. The dead are those who became Christians through receiving the gospel and eventually lost their lives through persecution inflicted by non-Christians.

Their judgment in the flesh by men lies in the past, but their lives in the spirit continue in a relationship with God. Their immaterial beings go on living in the presence of God as a result of having the gospel preached to them (4:6c). That furnishes the incentive to persevere in the face of the worst type of opposition. That is the ultimate victory for the one who died with Christ and who lives with Christ. Two options are open: one of living for the lusts of men and being judged by God and the other of living for the will of God and being judged by men before an ongoing life in the presence of God. The one who wants to enjoy victory as Christ did will always choose the latter option.

Paying the ultimate price to gain the ultimate victory
In 1997 I visited a village in Ukraine where a small group of Christians was converting a former Jewish synagogue into a church. At one time, years before, a vibrant church existed in that town. The church was thriving and winning many in the area to Christ, until governmental authorities of the communist regime decided that such a vibrant church was a threat to the philosophy they sought to instill in the people. The authorities began removing leaders in the church, one by one, and sending them to parts unknown, perhaps Siberia. They continued doing so until the church had no leaders left. The church died, leaving only two elderly ladies to pray that God would somehow bring the church back as a corporate testimony in their community. With the collapse of communism and the coming of freedom to that area in 1990, God answered their prayers. He sent a young man from nearby Odessa whose zeal for Christ brought many to Christ and revived the testimony of that church in the surrounding area.

The men who were removed by governmental authorities were never heard from again. They were husbands and fathers who left their wives and children behind and became victims of an unknown fate. In all probability they spent the rest of their lives in prison and died there. If they knew the message of 1 Peter 4:1-6, they were in all probability glad to give their lives, because they now enjoy an uninterrupted life in the presence of God. They were judged according to men in the flesh, but they now live according to God in the spirit. In the end, they and not their communist persecutors are the victors.

In other parts of the world, Christians are experiencing the same kind of treatment. We do not know how many will suffer a martyr's death. We do not know whether we will be called on to suffer the way others have. We do know, however, that 'unless a grain of wheat falls into the earth and dies, it remains alone; but if it dies, it bears much fruit' (John 12:24). We also know that we died with Christ with respect to sin and that we live with Christ with respect to righteousness. If our death with Him entails a path that leads to martyrdom, we should be willing to follow that path. Because of the assurance of 1 Peter 4:1-6, we know that our life with Christ will continue in spite of what the worst oppressor may do to us.

The following chart summarizes the discussion above and emphasizes the critical importance of the death-life paradox in Christian self-concept:

THE SAME MIND AS CHRIST

Matching Christ's Purpose		
He did nothing but good in living for the will of God (3:17)	He ceased from sin when He suffered and died for our sin (3:18)	He suffered for sins (3:18) and was resurrected (3:21)
resisting the lusts of men and living for the will of God (4:2)	ceasing from sin because of our death with Christ (4:1)	reckoning death and resurrection with Christ (4:1-2)

Matching Christ's Response		
He was willing to suffer for doing nothing but good and living for the will of God (3:17)	He was willing to give up His life at the hands of his persecutors (3:18)	He anticipated His ultimate victory at the right hand of God (3:22)
accepting harsh treatment because of living for the will of God (4:4)	willing to give up our lives to live for the will of God (4:6a)	anticipating future life with God after death (4:6b)

Chapter 16

CULTIVATING CHRISTIAN LOVE

1 John 3:14

1 John 3:14

We know that we have passed from death to life, because we love the brothers. The one who does not love abides in death.

John the Apostle, author of the Gospel of John, described one of the five occasions when Jesus spoke of the death-life paradox in Christian self-concept. That occasion came during Passion Week when some Greeks approached one of Jesus' disciples and asked to see Jesus. An earlier chapter in this work, the one dealing with living fruitfully for God (chapter 8), has described the details of that occasion. John 12:25 states most succinctly the principle set forth by Jesus at that time: 'The one who loves his life loses it, and the one who hates his life in this world will protect it to life eternal.' The text of John 12 does not explicitly place John the apostle and writer of the Gospel within earshot of Jesus when He spoke these words, but as our earlier discussion of that passage indicated, the context implies that the crowd standing nearby heard the words (John 12:28-29). The apostle most probably was in that crowd.

The same John wrote his first epistle a little over sixty years after receiving that principle from Jesus. The epistle divulges what impressions he developed in that long period of reflection about how Jesus had told His disciples to hate their lives in this world in order to protect their lives to life eternal. That lesson had a powerful impact on the beloved disciple as evidenced by a number of features of 1 John. John accepted the guideline as being so binding that he concluded that a professing Christian in violating that guideline was evidencing that his Christian profession was empty. The following connections between Jesus' command in John 12:25 and the first Johannine epistle will show how John received and over the years developed the lesson. Note the following elements from 1 John:

(1) John recognized that loving one's earthly, temporal life amounted to not having eternal life because that is the same as loving the world (1 John 2:15).

(2) He also indicated that hating one's earthly, temporal life, the opposite of loving the world and the things in it, amounted to protecting one's life to life eternal (1 John 2:17).

(3) In addition, not loving the world and the things that are in it, he wrote, equated to participating in the resurrection life of Jesus Christ Himself (1 John 1:1-2; 5:11-12, 20).

(4) Further, he noted that a love for Christian brothers evidences possession of that resurrection life (1 John 3:14-15).

Our discussion to follow elaborates on these four elements.

Hatred toward earthly, temporal life (John 12:25) = no love for the world (1 John 2:15-17)

Immediately after acknowledging his readers' forgiveness of sins, personal relationship with the Father and with the pre-existent Christ, and victory over the evil one (2:12-14), John commands them to 'stop loving the world and the things that are in it' (2:15a). Such a prohibition is surprising because the recipients of the command are a group of people whom the writer has just complimented for their positive spiritual achievements. That he would issue such a restriction is indicative that at least some of them had an affection for the world. He calls upon the 'world-lovers' to make a complete break with the world.

Determining what he means by 'world' is somewhat problematic. Does he mean the morally neutral world of people, the morally neutral world of material creation, the morally neutral world of people and material creation, or the morally evil world in its totality? Most probably, John intends the last of these meanings here. When he adds 'and the things that are in it,' he stipulates the ethical qualities that adhere to the objects of which the world consists. They are the elements that compose the earthly, temporal life, love for which Jesus said would exclude one from spiritual, eternal life (John 12:25).

Some have raised the relevant question of how to reconcile 1 John 2:15a with John 3:16, according to which we know that 'God so loved the world, that He gave His one and only Son, that whoever believes in Him should not perish, but have eternal life.' Why can God love the world but Christians cannot? Perhaps the answer lies in a different meaning for 'world' in John 3:16, the meaning of a world of morally neutral people. But also the answer may lie in the difference between God and man. Loving is a surrendering of oneself. Because of their depravity, when people surrender themselves to the world, the world sweeps them along with its waywardness and ruins them. When God surrenders Himself, He does so in order to save the world. His love is unmotivated by selfish interests, but the motivation of human love stems from desires for self-gratification. The believer needs to recognize those baser inclinations as having died when he died with Christ. That self-concept equates to hatred toward earthly, temporal life.

By listing the elements that compose what the world offers, 1 John 2:16 furnishes the reason why love for the world excludes the possibility of love for God. They are the lusts that the flesh and the eyes have and the pride that accompanies man's earthly life. John specifies that those sinful inclinations do not proceed from the Father, but from the world. The kinds of inclinations that stem from the Father are those that lead toward a relative disdain for what this world has to offer rather than a love for this earthly, temporal life. As Jesus said, 'The one who loves his life loses it, and the one who hates his life in this world will protect it. . . .' (John 12:25). In some cases that relative contempt for this earthly existence may bring with it a loss of physical life. That is what Jesus had in mind in speaking of a grain of wheat falling to the ground and dying in John 12:24. That sacrificial death was necessary for Him, and in some instances will be necessary for His disciples. First John 3:16 reiterates the same lesson when it recalls, 'He laid down His life for us, and we ought to lay down our lives for the brothers.' This is another reminder that death must precede life and fruitfulness.

Protecting one's life to life eternal (John 12:25) = doing the will of God (1 John 2:17)

Another seed-thought from Jesus' death-life paradox delivered during Passion Week relates to eternal life, about which John has much to say in his first epistle. In 1 John 2:17 he promises that the person who does the will of God abides forever. Abiding forever can mean nothing other than possessing eternal life. In the paragraph 2:15-17, doing the will of God (2:17b) must be the opposite of loving the world and the things that are in it (2:15a). Here is another way of stating the death-life paradox.

In 1 John 1:2 John wrote that he and the other apostles proclaimed to their readers eternal life, by which he meant life with eternal duration. That fits with his reference to abiding forever in 2:17b. In this instance, doing the will of God is the key to living forever. That will dictates how a believer should view his own relationship to the world as a non-relationship. In the emphasis of Paul and Peter, he/she has died with Christ when it comes to the things of this world. John notes Jesus' personal promise of eternal life in 1 John 2:25, a possible reference back to what Jesus promised about protecting one's life to life eternal in John's Gospel.

John's purpose in addressing this epistle to those who believe in the name of the Son of God was that he might reassure them about the promise of eternal life that Jesus left (1 John 5:13). On the negative side of the issue, when he stated that no murderer has eternal life abiding in him (1 John 3:16), he reminded his readers of the consequences of not repudiating this world with its earthly, temporal values. That person has not repudiated the things of this world and, therefore, does not possess eternal life.

John wove the lesson about eternal life that he learned from Jesus into the fabric of the epistle from beginning to end. In fact, he had the two parts of the death-life paradox—hatred for one's earthly, temporal life and protecting one's spiritual, eternal life—indelibly impressed upon his own mind and passed those impressions on to the readers of this first epistle.

Eternal life = the resurrection life of Christ himself (1 John 1:2; 5:12, 20)

Another element of Jesus' teaching in 1 John pertains to the nature of the life that Jesus promised. In John 11:25 Jesus told Martha, 'I am the resurrection and the life.' The life that Jesus promised in some sense is none other than Himself and His resurrection. The way that Paul developed that basic thought in Romans 6:1-11, Galatians 2:20, and elsewhere was to show that the 'life' side of the death-life paradox consisted of the resurrection life of Christ in which the believer shares. It is eternal in that Jesus will never die again, and because of their identification with Him Christians share that eternal life also. John was doubtless familiar with Paul's teaching on this subject by the time he wrote 1 John. Though he does not frame the thought in precisely the same way as Paul, he makes it quite clear that the eternal life that believers possess is none other that Christ Himself, in other words, they share Christ's resurrection life.

That equation between eternal life and Christ Himself is clear at several points in the epistle. First John 1:2 records John's testimony that he had seen the manifestation of the life. Clearly that statement on the heels of verse 1 regarding the hearing, seeing, beholding, and handling could refer to nothing other than his personal experience in the company of Jesus. Jesus is in some sense the eternal life that believers enjoy. The apostle probably did not at the time fathom the depth of Jesus' statement about being the resurrection and the life. Subsequent to His death and resurrection from the dead, however, he and others—including Paul—came to understand the truth about a believer's identification with Christ in His death and resurrection. That understanding undoubtedly lay behind John's statement of having seen the manifestation of life in His prolonged exposure to Jesus during His earthly ministry and his contacts with Him following His resurrection.

At the end of the epistle also John equates eternal life with Jesus Christ Himself. First John 5:20 has that equation: 'We know that the Son of God has come, and has given us understanding that we might know the true one; and we are in the true one, in His Son Jesus Christ. This is the true God and eternal life.' Debate centers around whether the 'this' in verse 20 refers to the Father or to His Son Jesus Christ. The fact that the epistle's second verse refers to Jesus as life is strong evidence for the latter identification, as is the proximity of 'this' to 'His Son Jesus Christ' at the end of the previous sentence.

But even if 5:20 does not equate Jesus with the eternal life He provides, 5:12 does make that association: 'The one who has the Son has life; the one who does not have the Son of God does not have life.' To have the Son is to have life because that He is life is a certainty. The inverse statement about the one who does not have the Son is also true. The equating of the Son with eternal life would have been impossible to understand before He rose from the dead. In the days of His incarnation He could promise eternal life as He did when He promised, 'The one who hates his life in this world will protect it to life eternal' (John 12:25). Even after His resurrection the concept combining His person with the substance of a promise of living forever is difficult, but this was John's way of expressing the 'life' part of the death-life paradox. He chose a different way of expressing the 'death' part of the paradox when he spoke of hating the world and the things that are in it (2:15). That use of hatred arose from the paradox spoken of by Jesus during the Passion Week in His encounter with the Greeks who wanted to see Him (John 12:25).

Once again, then, in 1 John we see the death-life paradox in Christian self-concept that Jesus initiated as it continues its impact on one of the Twelve into the last decade of the first century.

Love for Christian brothers as evidence of eternal Life (1 John 3:14-15)

One particular commentary on 1 John appropriately carries the title, *The Tests of Life*.[1] John offers a number of tests within the epistle, but the one that is relevant to our present discussion comes in 1 John 3:14-15: 'We know that we have passed from death into life, because we love the brothers; the one who does not love abides in death. Everyone who hates his brother is a murderer, and you know that no murderer has eternal life abiding in him.' Obviously the death spoken of here is spiritual death—the realm of sin, its punitive consequences, and its corruption. Its opposite is life, eternal life enjoyed by those who have the Son (5:12).

This test of faith consists of a self-examination to ascertain a person's relationship with fellow Christians. John presents only two alternatives: love and hate. Love for a brother demonstrates that a person dwells in the realm of spiritual, eternal life, i.e., the realm of the resurrection life of our Lord Jesus Christ. An absence of love which amounts to hatred indicates a person's alienation from God in the realm of spiritual death. Such a person has loved his life in this world (John 12:25a) and has retained his love for the world and the things that are in it (1 John 2:15). On the other hand, the one who loves his brother has hated his life in this world (John 12:25b) and withheld his love for the world (1 John 2:15).

John echoes other teachings of Jesus in 1 John 3:14-15. Specifically, he shows his recollection of John 13:34-35: 'I give you a new commandment, that you love one another, just as I have loved you, that you love one another. In this all will know that you are My disciples, if you have love for one another.' Keeping this

1. Robert Law, *The Tests of Life: A Study of the First Epistle of St. John* 'T. & T. Clark, 1909'.

command of the Lord is evidence that a person has adopted personally the death-life paradox that Jesus directed as a self-concept. That concept is the starting-point in being His disciple and will result in love for other disciples as a badge of that discipleship.

Another echo of Jesus' teaching lies in the equating of hatred with murder. In Matthew 5:21-22 Jesus taught, 'You have heard that it was said to those of old, "You shall not murder," and "whoever murders will be liable to judgment." But I say to you that everyone who is angry with his brother will be liable to judgment; and whoever says to his brother, "Raca," shall be liable to the Council; and whoever says, "Foolish one," shall be liable to Gehenna of fire.' In His Sermon on the Mount, Jesus taught that the motive behind one's actions, not overt action, is the ultimate source of divine concern. Anger and hatred toward a brother are tantamount to murder even though an evil intent may not be ultimately carried out. That is the thought behind John's words in 1 John 3:15 leading to the obvious observation that no murderer has eternal life abiding in him.

As was true in John's day, fellow Christians divide themselves into two categories: those who are easy to love and those who are hard to love. The true test of Christian love is an ability to love those in the latter category. That is the way God loved us. John reminds us, 'In this is love, not that we loved God, but that He Himself loved us and sent His Son as a propitiation for our sins' (1 John 4:10). He did not love us in return for our being easy to love. We were the very opposite when we rebelled against Him in our sinfulness. Yet He loved us in spite of our rebellion. That is the way we are to love our brothers in Christ, for John also reminds us that 'we love because He Himself first loved us' (1 John 4:19). In other words, we know the meaning of love because He gave us a demonstration of what love is by loving us first. We demonstrate that we have passed from spiritual death to eternal life by exercising that kind of love toward one another.

Both in theological circles where I spend most of my time and in local church situations, I am trying to learn the vital importance of love for brothers and sisters in Christ. Often exercising such love is not easy. In one instance, a leader in my church went to the highest officer in the institution where I was teaching to ask him to force me to refrain from filling a leadership role in my own church. The difficulty I had in loving that church leader after that is obvious. But I had to love him if I allowed the resurrected Christ to live His life through me. If I did not hate my earthly, temporal response to that situation, I would have hated the man.

In dialogue with professors at other theological institutions, language can at times become harsh when disagreements over biblical interpretation arise. At times, I have been accused of some very subversive actions. That has hurt deeply because I always try to operate on the highest of ethical planes. My earthly, temporal response to such false accusations would be to hate those who put such defamation in print, but I can't hate them. The resurrected Christ who lives His life through me can do only one thing, and that is to love them.

The sooner we Christians learn to think of ourselves as having died with Christ and as having been raised with Him, the sooner the world around us will get a taste of how the love of Christ functions in healing many of the world's wounds.

The following chart summarizes the discussion above and emphasizes the critical importance of the death-life paradox in Christian self-concept:

THE DEATH-LIFE PARADOX IN 1 JOHN

	Death	Life
How John's Gospel says it	Hatred toward earthly, temporal life (12:25)	Protecting one's life to life Eternal (12:25)
How 1 John says it	Hating the world and the things in it (2:15-17)	Doing the will of God, abiding forever (2:17)
How John's Gospel says it	Hatred toward earthly, temporal life (12:25)	I am the resurrection and the Life (11:25)
How 1 John says it	Hating the world and the things in it (2:15-17)	"His Son Jesus Christ" is "eternal life." (5:20); "The one who has the Son has life" (5:12)
How John's Gospel says it	Hatred toward earthly, temporal life (12:25)	"In this all will know that you are My disciples, if you have love for one another" (13:35)
How 1 John says it	Hating the world and the things in it (2:15-17)	"We know that we have passed from death into life because we love the brothers" (3:14)

Chapter 17

FACING
MARTYRDOM

Revelation 12:10-12

Revelation 12:10-12

[10]*And I heard a loud voice in heaven, saying, 'Now salvation and power and the kingdom of our God and the authority of His Christ have come, because the accuser of our brothers has been thrown down, the one who accused them before our God day and night.*

[11]*And they themselves overcame him because of the blood of the Lamb and because of the word of their testimony, and they did not love their life even to death. [12]On account of this, rejoice, O heavens and those who dwell in them. Woe to the earth and the sea, because the devil has come down to you, having great wrath, knowing that he has a short time.'*

We now turn from the past to the future in our survey of the death-life paradox in a Christian's view of self. One of the visions granted to John the apostle on the island of Patmos portrayed a great sign in heaven: a woman clothed with the sun, the moon under her feet, and twelve stars on her head (Rev. 12:1). In light of Genesis 37:9-11, the woman most probably symbolizes national Israel. The other character in the vision was a great, fiery-red dragon with seven heads and ten horns and seven crowns on his heads (Rev. 12:3). According to Revelation 12:9, the dragon undoubtedly represents Satan. The vision portrays Satan's persecution of Israel during the future three and one-half years (i.e., 1,260 days, Rev. 12:6) just before the return of Christ to earth.

Michael and his angels will prevail in warfare over Satan and cast Satan and his angels from heaven into the earth. A jubilant hymn, probably sung by saints in heaven (as in Rev. 6:10-11), celebrates the relocation of the devil from heaven to earth (Rev. 12:10-12). The hymn's three stanzas rejoice over the arrival of God's kingdom and Christ's authority (12:10), the earthly victory of the saints who identify with Christ in His witness and death (12:11), and the expulsion of the devil along with a warning to earth because of his ejection from heaven (12:12). A detailing of the three stanzas in reverse order will show the key importance to be played in the future celebration of Christ's ultimate victory by the self-concept of saints who are persecuted by Satan.

Celebration and warning over the devil's expulsion from heaven (12:12)

Satan is currently an unwelcome guest in heaven. God in His wisdom, for reasons we cannot understand, allows that great deceiver (see Rev. 12:9) access to His heavenly courts. The book of Job describes one occasion when Satan had a heavenly audience. Satan used the occasion to argue a case against Job by telling the Lord that Job was blameless and upright only because God had blessed him in so many material ways (Job 1:9-10). To prove Satan wrong about this man, God allowed Satan to afflict Job in various ways, first by taking his oxen and donkeys and slaying his servants (Job 1:14-15), then by burning his sheep and slaying more servants

(1:16), then by taking his camels and more servants (1:17), and then by killing his sons and daughters (1:18-19). In all this tragedy, however, Job did not sin or blame God (1:22). In response to a further request, the Lord permitted Satan to afflict Job with painful boils from head to foot (2:7). It was so bad that Job's wife encouraged him to curse God so that he could die and find relief from his misery (2:9), but Job maintained his integrity and did not sin against God with his lips (2:10).

Undoubtedly, Satan has through the centuries made life miserable for countless others among God's people through his accusations before God's throne in heaven. Note that Revelation 12:10 calls him 'the accuser of our brothers'—the 'our' shows that the singers of this hymn were also saints, not angels—and identifies him as 'the one who accuses them before our God day and night.' Any follower of Jesus Christ whose life is having an impact for righteousness and truth is a target of the devil, either directly and personally or indirectly through the devil's angels. Since he no longer has access to try and destroy the incarnate, virgin-born Son of God (see Rev. 12:4b-5), his only remaining recourse is to accuse the Son's followers before God and try to gain permission for making life as miserable for them as possible. If possible, he wants to deter their faithful witness for Christ and to impugn their integrity just as he tried to do with Job.

The heavens and the angels who dwell there will be called upon to rejoice in that future day when Michael and his forces cast the devil out from heaven (Rev. 12:12a). Heaven will be rid of that subversive element that always seeks to undercut God's people on earth through menacing accusations. Yet his departure from heaven will pose worse threats to his new locale—the earth—so the hymn pronounces a 'woe' on the earth and sea (Rev. 12:12b). He will no longer accuse saints before God, but he will vent his frustration by the outpouring of great wrath directly against saints alive at that time (Rev. 12:12c). He will know his time is short before the return of Christ. That awareness will heighten his efforts to wipe out all living testimony about the saving work of Christ at Calvary and about His resurrection and victory over the grave.

That wrath will translate into martyrdom for many of God's

people who inhabit the earth during those three and one-half years. Jesus referred to the period as the 'Great Tribulation' (Matt. 24:21) because of the misery brought by God's judgment against earth's rebels, but it will also mean tribulation for the saints by way of persecution inflicted by Satan's personal representatives. The beast from the sea and the beast from the earth will carry out the devil's will in inflicting misery on God's people (Rev. 13:7, 15). Many will die because of their faithfulness to Christ in those days.

The victory of saints over the devil (12:11)

Whether suffering as a result of Satan's heavenly accusations or his direct persecution on earth, God's people can win the victory, however. This heavenly hymn incorporates clues as to how that victory will be won for the future generation of saints as they undergo the severest of treatment that the devil can mete out. The triumph will come for them 'because of the blood of the Lamb and because of the word of their testimony' (12:11a). They will be victorious because the Lamb was victorious over the enemy. Christ said, 'I have overcome,' referring to His death, when He speaks of his own victory (Rev. 3:21; see John 16:33; Rev. 5:5, 9). That was the occasion when He 'disarmed rulers and authorities' and 'made a public display of them, triumphing over them by the cross' (Col. 2:15). Because of His victory at Calvary, Christ took His seat at the Father's right hand in heaven (Rev. 3:21; see Ps. 110:1; Matt. 22:44; Acts 2:34; Eph. 1:20; Heb. 1:3; 8:1; 10:12; 12:2). The blood of the Lamb will also be the primary means of victory for His saints too.

As already indicated, the sojourn of these saints on earth will come just before the inauguration of Christ's kingdom on earth. They will not be subject to heavenly accusation during that period, but will have endured it prior to that and must face the worst that the dragon—i.e., Satan (Rev. 12:9)— has to offer when he is forced to limit his presence to earth. For the saints designated in this hymn, martyrdom is still ahead as they enter the final period of Great Tribulation. The wrath of the dragon will pinpoint them as its victims. Their victory over him will come through the terrible experience of martyrdom. Though a physical setback, martyrdom will be a spiritual triumph because ultimately they will sit with Christ on His throne (Rev. 3:21).

The primary and objective cause of their victory is the blood of the Lamb, but Revelation 12:11 assigns a secondary and subjective cause also. 'The word of their testimony' (12:11) refers to their own personal labor and self-sacrifice. Because of the shedding of the Lamb's blood, they will have an answer to the accuser's charges, but in His death they also will find motivation to devote themselves to His service, a devotion that furnishes a secondary cause for their victory. 'The word of their testimony' is the word of God to which they have borne testimony. These saints will give faithful testimony and confession even to the point of death, thereby contributing to their own victory. In situations when they face martyrdom, they will deliver evangelistic confessions of Jesus in communicating the powerful word of God.

Basic to the noble response of these martyrs will be another factor, however: 'they did not love their life until death' (12:11). They conceive of themselves exactly the way Jesus taught that a person should think of himself when He said, 'the one who hates his life in this world will protect it to life eternal' (John 12:25b) and John, the writer of Revelation, recorded those words spoken by Jesus the week He was crucified. Matthew, Mark, and Luke recorded a similar statement of Jesus spoken earlier at Caesarea-Philippi: 'the one who loses his life for My sake will find it' (Matt. 16:25; see Mark 8:35; Luke 9:24). John had been present when Jesus enunciated that important principle on that earlier occasion as well as three other occasions described in the Gospels of Matthew and Luke (Matt. 10:39; Luke 14:26-27; 17:33). It is the same principle that Jesus exemplified in His own experience, that a grain of wheat must fall to the ground and die if it is to bear fruit (John 12:24). He 'humbled himself and became obedient to death—even death on a cross' (Phil. 2:8). It is the same attitude that Paul urged when he wrote, 'Contemplate this picture of yourself, that you died to sin and that you are alive to God because of your union with Christ Jesus' (see Rom. 6:11). It is a death-life paradox in how a Christian views himself.

It is the concept that Paul exemplified when he said to the

Ephesian elders, 'Neither do I count my life as dear to myself' (Acts 20:24a) and when he told the Christians at Caesarea, 'I am ready not only to be bound, but even to die at Jerusalem for the name of the Lord Jesus' (Acts 21:13). It was his attitude when he wrote, 'according to my earnest expectation and hope, . . . Christ shall even now, as always, be exalted in my body, whether by life or by death' (Phil. 1:20).

That same attitude toward self will sustain these future saints in the face of the worst that Satan can deal out. They will not love their lives to the point of death because they will consider themselves to have died already with Christ with reference to earthly, temporal values. Nothing the enemy can do to them in this life can cause them loss; they are already dead with Christ in that realm. As John recorded this prophetic vision of the heavenly hymn, he undoubtedly remembered what Jesus had taught him and the rest of the disciples. The equation of 'they did not love their life until death' in Revelation 12:11 with 'the one who hates his life in this world will protect it to life eternal' in John 12:25b is unmistakable. Though it is unstated in the hymn, the reward of protecting spiritual life that issues in eternal life must have crossed the apostle's mind. Though unstated, the wider context of the book of Revelation strongly implies that persecuted saints can endure anything and everything, including martyrdom, in their anticipation of their life with Christ after He returns. The thought of reigning with Christ in His kingdom (Rev. 20:4) and enjoying the bliss of the new Jerusalem (Rev. 21:1–22:5) must eventually have crossed John's mind as he recorded this hymn. That prospect is sufficient to maintain one's professed fidelity to Christ even if it entails a violent death. That anticipation will prompt these future saints to stand their ground against Satan, who as a punishment for their faithfulness to the Savior will take away their earthly, temporal lives.

Such people who willingly give their lives as martyrs to become testimonies for the sake of Christ will never be heroes in the eyes of their contemporaries. Their fellow citizens will probably look upon their deaths as good riddance. After all, the witnesses of Christ are a nuisance as long as they are around to remind others that rebellion against God can never succeed in the long run and that the fundamental need is to trust Christ and identify with Him despite the tremendous pressure to close ranks with others who live unrighteous lives. For resisting adverse pressure of this sort, saints of that future day will pay the price of their earthly lives, but will gain the victory of eternal life in God's presence.

Nor is that kind of pressure reserved for a future generation alone. Through John, Jesus wrote words of encouragement to a church at Smyrna (Rev. 2:8-11). It was a first-century church under severe affliction from Satan's representatives because of its testimony for Christ in that city. Christians in that church had already suffered and were about to suffer more when Christ wrote to them. They faced future imprisonment, stepped-up persecution, and eventually martyrdom if they refused to recant their allegiance to Jesus. Jesus' advice to them was to be faithful all the way to death, but along with that advice He promised them a crown that consists of eternal life (Rev. 2:10) and deliverance from the second death (Rev. 2:11). Loss of one's earthly, temporal life for a Christian is only a temporary setback. Believers have eternal life in God's new creation to look forward to after this life ends. The view of self that will sustain future followers of Christ is the same as that which sustains His present-day followers in the church.

The arrival of God's kingdom and Christ's authority (12:10)
The opening part of the hymn sung by saints in heaven celebrates the coming of 'the salvation and the power and the kingdom of our God and the authority of His Christ' (Rev. 12:10a). The 'salvation' that the singers celebrate speaks of the victory over the dragon, his casting from heaven being one more step in the establishment of God's kingdom on earth. The 'power' is God's power that achieved the great victory, the power operative throughout the victorious process. That power produced the male child and took Him to heaven (Rev. 12:5) and provided for the dragon's defeat (12:8-9). The arrival of 'the kingdom of our God' is the same arrival celebrated in an earlier heavenly song sung by loud voices in heaven: 'The kingdom of the world has become [that] of our Lord and of His Christ, and He will reign forever and ever' (Rev. 11:15).

It includes the future temporal phase of one-thousand years (Rev. 20:1-10) and the eternal phase that will never end (21:1–22:5). Heavenly voices are not the only ones who celebrate the final victory of God in His creation; we should join our earthly voices with theirs in joyous anthems of praise. We will some day join with the chorus of Revelation 19:6 in singing, 'Allelujah, for the Lord God omnipotent reigneth!' We can begin practicing for that heavenly choir now, because God's Word assures us that He will be the eventual victor.

The song in Revelation 12:10a continues to celebrate 'the authority of His Christ,' the same authority sung about in 11:15. God the Son will be the agent who rules in the future kingdom of God. The kingdom of God on earth has not yet arrived, because Satan the accuser still has access to heaven. The song looks forward to the consummation when Christ returns, a time when Satan has no further work to carry out either in heaven or on earth, a time when Christ's authority will be fully established and evident to all.

As I pen this chapter, I am reading in my newspaper about Christians on several small Indonesian islands in the south Pacific ocean. They live in the presence of threatened execution by Muslim extremists. One of them said, 'They said if we didn't convert to their religion, they would cut our throats.' Another Christian said, 'Anyone who doesn't want to be killed has to convert to Islam.' One report from the region indicated that two Christian teachers had been killed for refusing to convert to Islam. Thousands of Christians have lost their lives because of their faithfulness to Christ. Some professing Christians have yielded to the pressure to convert, but in doing so, have received unspeakably harsh physical mutilation from their Muslim captors.

Suffering for Christ and martyrdom is not limited to the past or to the future. It is a present reality in many parts of the world at present. You and I may live in circumstances that do not at present call on us to suffer extreme pain or martyrdom because of our faith in Christ, but our concept of ourselves as having died with Christ and having been raised with Him should equip us to go all the way to death if adverse circumstances should arise to challenge our faith. Our faithfulness to Him requires that kind of spiritual stamina. Like the saints in the future Great Tribulation, we need to refrain from loving our lives if testimony for Christ brings us to the place we have to die for Him.

The following chart summarizes the discussion above and emphasizes the critical importance of the death-life paradox in Christian self-concept:

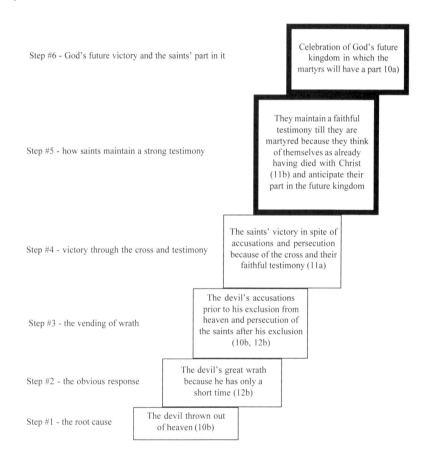

Step #6 - God's future victory and the saints' part in it

Celebration of God's future kingdom in which the martyrs will have a part 10a)

Step #5 - how saints maintain a strong testimony

They maintain a faithful testimony till they are martyred because they think of themselves as already having died with Christ (11b) and anticipate their part in the future kingdom

Step #4 - victory through the cross and testimony

The saints' victory in spite of accusations and persecution because of the cross and their faithful testimony (11a)

Step #3 - the vending of wrath

The devil's accusations prior to his exclusion from heaven and persecution of the saints after his exclusion (10b, 12b)

Step #2 - the obvious response

The devil's great wrath because he has only a short time (12b)

Step #1 - the root cause

The devil thrown out of heaven (10b)

Conclusion

THINKING OF OURSELVES
REALISTICALLY

We want to think about ourselves realistically, that is, in terms of who we really are. We don't want to imagine ourselves to be someone that we really aren't. We want our view of self to agree with facts. The best way we can do that is to see ourselves as God sees us. A believer is a person who has been born again and has trusted in Jesus Christ and His sacrifice to obtain eternal life and forgiveness of sins. The real identity of that believer includes his/her identification with Christ in His death on the cross and his/her identification with Christ in His resurrection from the dead. A believer is a living corpse, one who is dead in aspects of life that relate to pre-Christian existence and alive in aspects of existence that relate to the new person and the life of Christ within.

Often I have heard Christians speak of the need to crucify self. The Christian does not need to do that because he/she has already been crucified with Christ. He needs only to keep his co-crucifixion with Christ on his mind along with his co-resurrection with Christ. Constant recollection of those two facts will enable Christians to put to death 'the members [sinful deeds] which are upon the earth' (Col. 3:5) and to seek 'the things that are above' (Col. 3:1).

This death-life paradox in Christian self-concept is the plain teaching of the New Testament from beginning to end. Yet it is one of the best-kept secrets among Bible students. Jesus inaugurated the line of teaching during His earthly ministry and the apostles continued and developed it through the rest of the New Testament. The following chart reflects the chronological order in which the speakers/writers taught the death-life paradox, along with locations, circumstances, specific subjects, Scripture excerpts, and Scripture references.

Throughout the first century of Christianity, this way of viewing self permeated Christian thinking.

SUMMARY OF TEACHINGS ABOUT CONTEMPLATING OUR DEATH AND RESURRECTION WITH CHRIST

Speaker/ Writer	Date/Period	Subject	Scripture Excerpt	Passage Reference
Jesus	Winter, A.D. 29/ 16-month Ministry in Galilee	'Evaluating Family Ties'	'the one who loses his life for My sake will find it'	Mt 10:37-39
Jesus	Summer, A.D. 29/16- month Ministry around Galilee	'Suffering with Christ'	"whoever loses his life for My sake will find it"	Mt 16:24-26 etc.
Jesus	Winter, A.D. 30/3-month Ministry in and around Perea	'Evaluating Earthly Possessions'	"carry his own cross and come after Me"	Lk 14:26-27
Jesus	Winter, A.D. 30/3-month Ministry in and around Perea	'Evaluating the World's Allurements'	"whoever loses it shall preserve it alive"	Lk 17:32-33
Jesus	Spring, A.D. 30/ Passion Week	"Fruit-bearing for God"	'the one who hates his life ... will keep it to life eternal'	Jn 12:24-26
Paul	A.D. 55/Third Missionary Journey	'Failing Successfully'	'carrying ... the dying of Jesus, that the life of Jesus also my be manifested'	2 Cor 4:7-15
Paul	A.D. 55/Third Missionary Journey	'Persuading Others to Believe'	'all died; ... those who live'	2 Cor 5:11-21
Paul	A.D. 55/Third Missionary Journey	'Overcoming Sin's Domination'	'dead to sin, but alive to God'	Rom 6:1-14
Paul	A.D. 55/Third Missionary Journey	'Fulfilling Responsibilities'	'present your bodies a living sacrifice'	Rom 12:1-2
Paul	A.D. 56/Third Missionary Journey	'Gaining Freedom'	'crucified with Christ ... Christ lives in me'	Gal 2:19-20
Paul	A.D. 60/ First Roman Imprisonment	'Ridding Oneself of the Past'	"lay aside the old man ... put on the new man"	Eph 4:17-24
Paul	A.D. 60/ First Roman Imprisonment	'Counteracting Wrong Rules'	"you died with Christ ... you were raised with Christ"	Col 2:20-3:4
Paul	A.D. 60/ First Roman Imprisonment	'Succeeding Successfully'	'the power of His resurrection ... being conformed to His death'	Php 3:2-16
Peter	A.D. 65/ from Babylon	'Achieving Submission'	'"we, having died to sin, might live to righteousness'	1 Pet 2:24
Peter	A.D. 65/ from Babylon	'Following God's Will'	'the one who has suffered in the flesh ... that he may live'	1 Pet 4:1-6
John	A.D. 90/ from Ephesus	'Cultivating Love'	'we have passed from death to life'	1 Jn 3:14
John	A.D. 90/ from Ephesus	'Facing Martyrdom'	'they did not love their life even to death'	Rev 12:11

Jesus prepared His followers for this line of teaching before His death and resurrection by speaking to them in terms of losing one's life for His sake in order to find it. After His death and resurrection Paul picked up the theme when he advocated thinking about oneself as having died and having risen with Christ in His death and resurrection. Peter spoke of Christians as having died to sin so that they could live for righteousness. John reverted back to Jesus' teaching more directly by speaking of not loving the world and the things in it and doing the will of God in order to abide forever.

An ability to think of oneself in those terms lies at the foundation of lasting dedication to God. Any other view of self dooms a person to what is at best a short-lived yieldedness to God. To speak of being a disciple of Jesus Christ in any other terms is futile.

God sees us in that way. We need to agree with God that such is our true identity. That is how to think realistically about ourselves. There is no more compelling example of a human being who thought of himself in these terms than the apostle Paul, who wrote, 'I have been crucified with Christ, and I no longer live, but Christ lives in me' (Gal. 2:20a). That view of self served as the basis for his dedication to God and His will. Look what the Lord was able to accomplish through Paul's life. May Paul be our example in thinking of ourselves in the right way and in an unreserved dedication to Jesus Christ and His will.

In writing 'Moment by Moment,' the gospel-song writer captured the essence of the death-life paradox in Christian self-concept:

Dying with Jesus by death reckoned mine,
Living with Jesus a new life divine,
Looking to Jesus till glory doth shine,
Moment by moment, O Lord, I am thine.

Such a moment-by-moment reckoning of who I am as God sees me helps me maintain an awareness of the One to whom I belong. This is the high point in Christian living. This is the realistic Christian view of self and the one that places me completely at the disposal of my Lord and Savior.

Christian Focus Publications

We publish books for all ages. Our mission statement -

STAYING FAITHFUL
In dependence upon God we seek to help make his infallible word, the Bible, relevant. Our aim is to ensure that the Lord Jesus Christ is presented as the only hope to obtain forgiveness of sin, live a useful life and look forward to heaven with him.

REACHING OUT
Christ's last command requires us to reach out to our world with his gospel. We seek to help fulfil that by publishing books that point people towards Jesus and for them to develop a Christ-like maturity. We aim to equip all levels of readers for life, work, ministry and mission.

Books in our adult range are published in three imprints.

Christian Focus contains popular works including biographies, commentaries, basic doctrine, and Christian living. Our children's books are also published in this imprint.
Christian Heritage contains classic writings from the past.
Mentor focuses on books written at a level suitable for Bible College and seminary students, pastors, and other serious readers; the imprint includes commentaries, doctrinal studies, examination of current issues, and church history.

For a free catalogue of all our titles, please write to:

Christian Focus Publications, Ltd
Geanies House, Fearn,
Ross-shire, IV20 1TW, Scotland,
United Kingdom
info@christianfocus.com

For details of our titles visit us on our website
www.christianfocus.com